A Poetics

Charles Bernstein

This rich collection is far more than an important work of criticism by an extraordinary poet; it is a poetic intervention into criticism. "Artifice of Absorption," a key essay, is written in verse, and its structures and rhythms initiate the reader into the strength and complexity of the argument. *A Poetics* is part criticism and part poetry, part tract and part song, with no dull moments. $34.95 cloth/$15.95 paper

Hermes' Dilemma and Hamlet's Desire

On the Epistemology of Interpretation

Vincent Crapanzano

A distinguished anthropologist and a creative force behind postmodern writing in his field, Vincent Crapanzano here focuses his critical powers upon how the human sciences, particularly anthropology and psychoanalysis, articulate their fields of study. Treating subjects as diverse as Roman carnivals and spirit possession in Morocco, he looks critically at the inner workings of interpretation in the human sciences and literary study. $45.00 cloth/$16.95 paper

His Other Half

Men Looking at Women through Art

Wendy Lesser

"A model of the kind of flexible, interdisciplinary culture criticism that is desperately needed to bridge the gap between the general reader and the academic ghetto."

—*Washington Post Book World*

11 halftones/$12.95 paper

Playing in the Dark

Whiteness and the Literary Imagination

Toni Morrison

photo by Brian Lanker

Toni Morrison brings the genius of a master writer to this personal inquiry into the significance of African-Americans in the American literary imagination. Her compelling point is that the central characteristics of American literature—individualism, masculinity, the insistence upon innocence coupled to an obsession with figurations of death and hell—are responses to a dark and abiding Africanist presence.

William E. Massey Sr. Lectures in the History of American Civilization $14.95 cloth

Subversive Intent

Gender, Politics, and the Avant-Garde

Susan Rubin Suleiman

"Well aware of the manifold ironies that attend the notion of an avant-garde tradition, Suleiman carefully deconstructs many of the paradoxes that accompany such a presumably radical enterprise...A deep and moving insight."

—*New York Times Book Review*

15 halftones/$12.95 paper

Harvard University Press

Cambridge, MA 02138 (617) 495-2480

First winner of the Annual North American Indian Prose Award

Claiming Breath

Diane Glancy

Claiming Breath is the diary of one year, from December to December. It is, writes the author, "a winter count of sorts, a calendar, a diary of personal matters . . . and a final acceptance of a broken past."

0-8032-2140-1, $15.95

"This is a major work, exploring and illuminating territory that is both new and ancient; it's a wondrous illumination of the territory . . . in all its grief, wonder, delight, and obscurity." – Paula Gunn Allen

At bookstores or the University of Nebraska Press · 901 N 17 · Lincoln 68588-0520 · (800) 755-1105 publishers since 1941

GRAND STREET

41

Cover: Jean Tinguely, printed silk scarf (detail), 1978.

Grand Street is set in New Caledonia by T$_{E}$X Source, Houston, Tex., and printed by W. E. Barnett & Associates, Houston, Tex. Color separations and halftones are by Color Separations, Inc., Houston, Tex.

Grand Street (ISSN 0734-5496; ISBN 0-393-30826-X) is published quarterly by Grand Street Press (a project of the New York Foundation for the Arts, Inc., a not-for-profit corporation), 131 Varick Street, #906, New York, N.Y. 10013. Contributions and gifts to Grand Street Press, a project of the New York Foundation for the Arts, Inc., are tax-deductible to the extent allowed by law.

Unsolicited material should be addressed to the editors at *Grand Street*, 131 Varick Street, #906, New York, N.Y. 10013. Manuscripts will not be returned unless accompanied by a stamped, self-addressed envelope.

Second-class postage at New York, N.Y., and additional mailing offices. Postmaster: Please send address changes to Subscription Service, Dept. GRS, P.O. Box 3000, Denville, N.J. 07834.

Subscription orders and address changes should be addressed to Subscription Service, Dept. GRS, P.O. Box 3000, Denville, N.J. 07834. Subscriptions are $24 a year (four issues). Foreign subscriptions (including Canada) are $34 a year, and must be payable in U.S. funds. Single-copy price is $8.50. *Grand Street* is distributed to the trade by W. W. Norton & Company, 500 Fifth Avenue, New York, N.Y. 10110, and to newsstands only by B. DeBoer, Inc., 113 E. Centre St., Nutley, N.J. 07110.

GRAND STREET

Editor

Jean Stein

Managing Editor

Brooke Allen

Art Editor

Walter Hopps

Poetry Editor

Erik Rieselbach

Designer

Don Quaintance

Assistant Editors

Paige Crowley

Lee Smith

Production Assistant

Elizabeth Frizzell

Copy Editor

Kate Norment

Advertising Director

Chris Calhoun

Contributing Editors

Morgan Entrekin, Raymond Foye, Jonathan Galassi,
Andrew Kopkind, Alberto Manguel, Edward W. Said,
Robert Scheer, Jean Strouse, Jeremy Treglown,
Katrina vanden Heuvel, Shelley Wanger, Drenka Willen

Publishers

Jean Stein & Torsten Wiesel

CONTENTS

Incidents at the Shrine

Anderson had been waiting for something to fall on him. His anxiety was such that for the first time in several years he went late to work. It was just his luck that the Head of Department had chosen that day for an impromptu inspection. When he got to the museum he saw that his metal chair had been removed from its customary place. The little stool on which he rested his feet after running endless errands was also gone. His official messenger's uniform had been taken off the hook. He went to the main office and was told by one of the clerks that he had been sacked and that the supervisor was not available. Anderson started to protest, but the clerk got up and pushed him out of the office.

He went aimlessly down the corridors of the Department of Antiquities. He stumbled past the visitors to the museum. He wandered amongst the hibiscus and bougainvillea. He didn't look at the ancestral stoneworks in the museum field. Then he went home, dazed, confused by objects, convinced that he saw many fingers pointing at him. He went down streets he had never seen in his life and he momentarily forgot where his compound was.

When he got home he found that he was trembling. He was hungry. He hadn't eaten that morning and the cupboard was empty of food. He couldn't stop thinking about the loss of his job. Anderson had suspected for some time that the supervisor had been planning to give his job to a distant relation. That was the reason why the supervisor was always berating him on the slightest pretext. Seven years in the city had begun to make Anderson feel powerless because he didn't belong to the important societies and didn't have influential relatives. He spent the afternoon thinking about his condition in the world. He fell asleep and dreamt about his dead parents.

He woke up feeling bitter. It was late in the afternoon and he was hungry. He got out of bed and went to the market to get some beef and tripe for a pot of stew. Anderson slid through the noise of revving motors and shouting traders. He came to the goatsellers. The goats stood untethered in a small corral. As Anderson went past he had a queer feeling that the goats were staring at him. When he stopped and looked at them, the animals panicked. They kicked and fought backwards. Anderson hurried on till he found himself at the meat stalls.

The air was full of flies and the stench was overpowering. He felt ill. There were intestines and bones in heaps on the floor. He was haggling the price of tripe when he heard confused howls from the section where they sold generators and videos. The meat-seller had just slapped the tripe down on the table and was telling him to go somewhere else for the price he offered, when the fire burst out with an explosion. Flames poured over the stalls. Waves of screaming people rushed in Anderson's direction. He saw the fire flowing behind them, he saw black smoke. He started to run before the people reached him.

He heard voices all around him. Dry palm fronds crackled in the air. Anderson ducked under the bare eaves of a stall, tripped over a fishmonger's basin of writhing eels, and fell into a mound of snailshells. He struggled back up. He ran past the fortune-tellers and the amulet traders. He was shouldering his way through the bamboo poles of the lace-sellers when it struck him with amazing clarity that the fire was intent upon him because he had no power to protect himself. And soon the fire was everywhere. Suddenly, from the midst of voices in the smoke, Anderson heard someone calling his names. Not just the one name, the ordinary one which made things easier in the city—Anderson; he heard all the others as well, even the ones he had forgotten: Jeremiah, Ofuegbu, Nutcracker, Azzi. He was so astonished that when he cut himself by brushing his thigh against two rusted nails, he did not know how profusely he bled till he cleared out into the safety of the main road. When he got home he was still bleeding. When the bleeding ceased, he felt that an alien influence had insinuated itself into his body, and an illness took over.

He became so ill that most of the money he had saved in all the years of humiliation and sweat went into the hands of the quack chemists of the area. They bandaged his wound. They gave him tetanus injections with curved syringes. They gave him pills in squat, silvery bottles. Anderson was reduced to creeping about the compound, from room to toilet and back again, as though he were terrified of daylight. And then, three days into the illness, with the taste of alum stale in his mouth, he caught a glimpse of himself in the mirror. He saw the gaunt face of a complete stranger. Two days later, when he felt he had recovered sufficiently, Anderson packed his box and fled home to his village.

The Image-maker

Anderson hadn't been home for a long time. When the lorry driver dropped him at the village junction, the first things he noticed were the ferocity of the heat and the humid smell of rotting vegetation. He went down the dirt track that led to the village. A pack of dogs followed him for a short while and then disappeared. Cowhorns and the beating of drums sounded from the forest. He saw masks, eaten by insects, along the grass verge.

He was sweating when he got to the obeche tree where, during the war, soldiers had shot a woman thought to be a spy. Passing the well which used to mark the village boundary, he became aware of three rough forms running after him. They had flaming red eyes and they shouted his names.

"Anderson! Ofuegbu!"

He broke into a run. They bounded after him.

"Ofuegbu! Anderson!"

In his fear he ran so hard that his box flew open. Scattered behind him were his clothes, his medicines, and the modest gifts he had brought to show his people that he wasn't entirely a small man in the world. He discarded the box and sped on without looking back. Swirls of dust came towards him. And when he emerged from the dust, he saw the village.

It was sunset. Anderson didn't stop running till he was safely in the village. He went on till he came to the pool office with the signboard that read: MR. ABAS AND CO. LICENSED COLLECTOR. Outside the office, a man sat in a depressed cane chair. His eyes stared divergently at the road and he snored gently. Anderson stood panting. He wanted to ask directions to his uncle's place, but he didn't want to wake the owner of the pool office.

Anderson wasn't sure when the man woke up, for suddenly he said: "Why do you have to run into our village like a madman?"

Anderson struggled for words. He was sweating.

"You disturb my eyes when you come running into our village like that."

Anderson wiped his face. He was confused. He started to apologize, but the man looked him over once, and fell back into sleep, with his eyes still open. Anderson wasn't sure what to do. He was thirsty. With sweat dribbling down his face, Anderson tramped on through the village.

Things had changed since he'd been away. The buildings had lost their individual colors to that of the dust. Houses had moved several yards from where they used to be. Roads ran diagonally to how he remembered them. He felt he had arrived in a place he had almost never known.

Exhausted, Anderson sat on a bench outside the market. The roadside was full of ants. The heat mists made him sleepy. The market behind him was empty, but deep within it he heard celebrations and arguments. He listened to alien voices and languages from the farthest reaches of the world. Anderson fell asleep on the bench and dreamt that he was being carried through the village by the ants. He woke to find himself inside the pool office. His legs itched.

The man whom he had last seen sitting in the cane chair was

now behind the counter. He was mixing a potion of local gin and herbs. There was someone else in the office: a stocky man with a large forehead and a hardened face.

He stared at Anderson and then said: "Have you slept enough?"

Anderson nodded. The man behind the counter came round with a tumbler full of herbal mixtures.

Almost forcing the drink down Anderson's throat, he said: "Drink it down. Fast!"

Anderson drank most of the mixture in one gulp. It was very bitter and bile rushed up in his mouth.

"Swallow it down!"

Anderson swallowed. His head cleared a little and his legs stopped itching.

The man who had given him the drink said: "Good." Then he pointed to the other man and said: "That's your uncle. Our Image-maker. Don't you remember him?"

Anderson stared at the Image-maker's face. The lights shifted. The face was elusively familiar. Anderson had to subtract seven years from the awesome starkness of the Image-maker's features before he could recognize his own uncle.

Anderson said: "My uncle, you have changed!"

"Yes, my son, and so have you," his uncle said.

"I'm so happy to see you," said Anderson.

Smiling, his uncle moved into the light at the doorway. Anderson saw that his left arm was shriveled.

"We've been expecting you," his uncle said.

Anderson didn't know what to say. He looked from one to the other. Then suddenly he recognized Mr. Abas, who used to take him fishing down the village stream.

"Mr. Abas! It's you!"

"Of course it's me. Who did you think I was?"

Anderson stood up.

"Greetings, my elders. Forgive me. So much has changed."

His uncle touched him benevolently on the shoulder and said: "That's all right. Now, let's go."

Anderson persisted with his greeting. Then he began to apologize for his bad memory. He told them that he had been pursued at the village boundary.

"They were strange people. They pursued me like a common criminal."

The Image-maker said: "Come on. Move. We don't speak of strange things in our village. We have no strange things here. Now, let's go."

Mr. Abas went outside and sat in his sunken cane chair. The Image-maker led Anderson out of the office.

They walked through the dry heat. The chanting of worshippers came from the forest. Drums and jangling bells sounded faintly in the somnolent air.

"The village is different," Anderson said.

The Image-maker was silent.

"What has happened here?"

"Don't ask questions. In our village we will provide you with answers before it is necessary to ask questions," the Image-maker said with some irritation.

Anderson kept quiet. As they went down the village Anderson kept looking at the Image-maker: the more he looked, the more raw and godlike the Image-maker seemed. It was as though he had achieved an independence from human agencies. He looked as if he had been cast in rock and left to the wilds.

"The more you look, the less you see," the Image-maker said.

It sounded, to Anderson, like a cue. They had broken into a path. Ahead of them were irregular rows of soapstone monoliths. Embossed with abstract representations of the human figure, the monoliths ranged from the babies of their breed to the abnormally large ones. There were lit candles and varied offerings in front of them. There were frangipani and iroko trees in their midst. There were also red-painted poles which had burst into flower.

His uncle said: "The images were originally decorated with pearls, lapis lazuli, amethysts, and magic glass which twinkled wonderful philosophies. But the pale ones from across the seas came and stole them. This was whispered to me in a dream."

Anderson gazed at the oddly elegant monoliths and said: "You resemble the gods you worship."

His uncle gripped him suddenly.

"We don't speak of resemblances in our village, you hear?"

Anderson nodded. His uncle relaxed his grip. They moved on.

After a while his uncle said: "The world is the shrine and the shrine is the world. Everything must have a center. When you talk rubbish, bad things fly into your mouth."

They passed a cluster of huts. Suddenly the Image-maker bustled forward. They had arrived at the main entrance to a circular clay shrinehouse. The Image-maker went to the niche and brought out a piece of native chalk, a tumbler, and a bottle of herbs. He made a mash which he smeared across Anderson's forehead. On a nail above the door, there was a bell which the Image-maker rang three times.

A voice called from within the hut.

The Image-maker sprayed himself forth in a list of his incredible names and titles. Then he requested permission to bring to the shrine an afflicted "son of the soil."

The voices asked if the "son of the soil" was ready to come in.

The Image-maker was silent.

A confusion of drums, bells, cowhorns, came suddenly from within. Anderson fainted.

Then the Image-maker said to the voices: "He is ready to enter!"

They came out and found that Anderson was light. They bundled him into the shrinehouse and laid him on a bed of congealed palm oil.

The Image

When Anderson came to, he could smell burning candles, sweat, and incense. Before him was the master Image, a hallucinatory warrior monolith decorated in its original splendor of precious stones and twinkling glass. At its base were roots, kola nuts, and feathers. When Anderson gazed at the master Image he heard voices that were not spoken and he felt drowsiness come over him.

Candles burned in the mist of blue incense. A small crowd of worshippers danced and wove Anderson's names in songs. Down the corridors he could hear other supplicants crying out in prayer for their heart's desires, for their afflictions and problems. They prayed like people who are ill and who are never sure of recovering. It occurred to Anderson that it must be a cruel world to demand such intensity of prayer.

Anderson tried to get up from the bed but couldn't. The master Image seemed to look upon him with a grotesque face. The ministrants closed in around him. They praised the master Image in songs. The Image-maker gave a sudden instruction and the ministrants rushed to Anderson. They spread out their multiplicity of arms and embraced Anderson in their hard compassions. But when they touched Anderson, he screamed and shouted in hysteria. The ministrants embraced him with their remorseless arms and carried him through the corridors and out into the night. They rushed him past the monoliths outside. They took him past creeks and waterholes. When they came to a blooming frangipani tree, they dumped him on the ground. Then they retreated with flutters of their smocks and disappeared, as though the darkness were made of their own substance.

Anderson heard whispers in the forest. He heard things falling among the branches. Then he heard footsteps that seemed for ever approaching. He soon saw that it was Mr. Abas. He carried a bucket in one hand and a lamp in the other. He dropped the bucket near Anderson.

"Bathe of it," Mr. Abas said, and returned the way he had come.

Anderson washed himself with the treated water. When he finished, the attendants came and brought him fresh clothes. Then they led him back to the shrinehouse.

The Image-maker was waiting for him. Bustling with urgency, his bad arm moving restlessly like the special instrument of his functions, the Image-maker grabbed Anderson and led him to an alcove.

He made Anderson sit in front of a door. There was a hole greased with palm oil at the bottom of the door. The Image-maker shouted an instruction and the attendants came upon

Anderson and held him face down. They pushed him towards the hole; they forced his head and shoulders through it.

In the pain Anderson heard the Image-maker say: "Tell us what you see!"

Anderson couldn't see anything. All he could feel was the grinding pain. Then he saw a towering tree. There was a door on the tree trunk. Then he saw a thick blue pall. A woman emerged from the pall. She was painted over in native chalk. She had bangles all the way up her arms. Her stomach and waist were covered in beads.

"I see a woman," he cried.

Several voices asked: "Do you know her?"

"No."

"Is she following you?"

"I don't know."

"Is she dead?"

"I don't know."

"Is she dead?"

"No!"

There was the merriment of tinkling bells.

"What is she doing?"

She had come to the tree and opened the door. Anderson suffered a fresh agony. She opened a second door and tried the third one, but it didn't open. She tried again and when it gave way with a crash Anderson finally came through—but he lost consciousness.

Afterwards, they fed him substantially. Then he was allowed the freedom to move round the village and visit some of his relations. In the morning the Image-maker sent for him. The attendants made him sit on a cowhide mat and they shaved off his hair. They lit red and green candles and made music around him. Then the Image-maker proceeded with the extraction of impurities from his body. He rubbed herbal juices into Anderson's shoulder. He bit into the flesh and pulled out a rusted little padlock, which he spat into an enamel bowl. He inspected the padlock. After he had washed out his mouth, he bit into Anderson's shoulder again and pulled out a crooked needle. He continued like this till he had pulled out a piece of broken glass, a twisted nail, a cowrie, and a small key. There was some agitation as to whether the key would fit the padlock, but it didn't.

When the Image-maker had finished, he picked up the bowl, jangled the objects, and said: "All these things, where do they come from? Who sent them into you?"

Anderson couldn't say anything.

The Image-maker went on to cut light razor strokes on Anderson's arm and he rubbed protective herbs into the bleeding marks. He washed his hands and went out of the alcove. He came back with a pouch, which he gave to Anderson with precise instructions of its usage.

Then he said: "You are going back to the city tomorrow. Go to your place of work, collect the money they are owing you, and look for another job. You will have no trouble. You understand?"

Anderson nodded.

"Now, listen. One day I went deep into the forest because my arm hurt. I injured it working in a factory. For three days I was in the forest praying to our ancestors. I ate leaves and fishes. On the fourth day I forgot how I came there. I was lost and everything was new to me. On the fifth day I found the Images. They were hidden amongst the trees and tall grasses. Snakes and tortoises were all around. My pain stopped. When I found my way back and told the elders of the village what I had seen, they did not believe me. The Images had been talked about in the village for a long time, but no one had actually seen them. That is why they made me the Image-maker."

He paused, then continued.

"Every year, around this time, spirits from all over the world come to our village. They meet at the marketplace and have heated discussions about everything under the sun. Sometimes they gather round our Images outside. On some evenings there are purple mists round the iroko tree. At night we listen to all the languages, all the philosophies, of the world. You must come home now and again. This is where you derive power. You hear?"

Anderson nodded. He hadn't heard most of what was said. He had been staring at the objects in the enamel bowl.

The Image-eaters

Anderson ate little through the ceremonies that followed the purification of his body. After all the dancing and feasting to the music of cowhorns and tinkling bells, they made him lie down before the master Image. Then the strangest voice he had ever heard thundered the entire shrinehouse with its full volume.

"ANDERSON! OFUEGBU! YOU ARE A SMALL MAN. YOU CANNOT RUN FROM YOUR FUTURE. GOVERNMENTS CANNOT EXIST WITHOUT YOU. ALL THE DISASTERS OF THE WORLD REST ON YOU AND HAVE YOUR NAME. THIS IS YOUR POWER."

The ministrants gave thanks and wept for joy.

Anderson spent the night in the presence of the master Image. He dreamt that he was dying of hunger and that there was nothing left in the world to eat. When Anderson ate of the master Image he was surprised at its sweetness. He was surprised also that the Image replenished itself.

In the morning Anderson's stomach was bloated with an imponderable weight. Shortly before his departure the Image-maker came to him and suggested that he contribute to the shrine fund. When Anderson made his donation, the Image-maker gave his blessing. The ministrants prayed for him and sang of his destiny.

Anderson had just enough money to get him back to the city. When he was ready to leave, Anderson felt a new heaviness come upon him. He thanked his uncle for everything and made his way through the village.

He stopped at the pool office. Mr. Abas was in his sunken cane chair, his eyes pursuing their separate lines of vision. Anderson wasn't sure if Mr. Abas was asleep.

He said: "I'm leaving now."

"Leaving us to our hunger, are you?"

"There is hunger where I am going," Anderson said.

Mr. Abas smiled and said: "Keep your heart pure. Have courage. Suffering cannot kill us. And travel well."

"Thank you."

Mr. Abas nodded and soon began to snore. Anderson went on towards the junction.

As he walked through the heated gravity of the village, Anderson felt like an old man. He felt that his face had stiffened. He had crossed the rubber plantation, had crossed the boundary, and was approaching the junction when the rough forms with blazing eyes fell upon him. He fought them off. He lashed out with his stiffened hands and legs. They could easily have torn him to pieces, because their ferocity was greater than his. There was a moment in which he saw himself dead. But they suddenly stopped and stared at him. Then they pawed him, as though he had become allied with them in some way. When they melted back into the heat mists, Anderson experienced the new simplicity of his life and continued with his journey.

Motets

Sobre el volcán la flor.
—G. A. Bécquer

You know: I'm going to lose you again
and I can't. Each action, every shout
jars me like a perfect shot,
even the salt breeze that floods the wharves,
breeding the dark spring
of Sottoripa.

Land of ironwork and mast
forests in the evening dust.
A long drone enters from outside,
torments like a fingernail on glass.
I'm after the lost sign, the one
pledge I had from you.
                         And hell is certain.

• • •

Long years, and one more difficult
above the foreign lake the sunsets burn on.
Then you came down from the hills to bring me back
Saint George and the Dragon.

If only I could print them on the banner
dancing to the whiplash of the heart's
east wind . . . And then descend for you
in eddying fidelity, immortal.

• • •

Frost on the windowpanes; the sick,
forever together, and apart;
and endless soliloquies
at the tables over the cards:

your exile. I remember mine,
the mornings when
I heard the ballerina
bomb ricochet in the rocks.

And the nightlong fireworks went on
and on, as at a party.

A harsh wing showed, and sheared your hands,
to no avail: it's not your card.

· · ·

Distant, I was with you when your father
went into shadow, leaving his farewell.
What did I know till then? The wearing-down
of *earlier* spared me for this alone:

that I didn't know you and should have;
by today's blows I do, if an hour
from down there bends back, bringing me
Cumerlotti or Anghébeni—to exploding mines
and moans and the advancing of the squadrons.

· · ·

Farewells, whistling in the dark, waves, coughs,
and lowered windows. It's time.
Maybe the robots have it right.
Look how they look from the corridors, boxed in!

. . .

—Do you too lend
your train's faint hymn
this awful, faithful carioca rhythm?—

• • •

The hope of even seeing you again
was leaving me;

and I asked myself if this which closes off
all sense of you from me, this screen of images,
is marked by death, or if, out of the past,
though twisted and diminished, it retains
some flash *of yours:*

(under the arcades, at Modena,
a servant wearing gold braid led
two jackals on a leash).

• • •

The black-and-white sine wave
of the martins from the telegraph
pole to the sea
doesn't comfort your suffering on the pier
or bring you back where you no longer are.

Already the elder sends its thick perfume
across the pit; the squall fans out.
If the brightness is a truce,
your sweet threat consumes it.

• • •

Here's the sign: it quivers on
the wall turning to gold:
a palm-leaf crenellation
burned by the dazzle of dawn.

The step that arrives
from the greenhouse so faint
isn't felted with snow: it's still
your life, your blood in my veins.

• • •

The green lizard, if it darts
out of the stubble
under the huge scythe—

the sail, when it luffs
and dives at the jolt
of the rock—

the noon cannon
fainter than your heart,
and the stopwatch that sounds
without a sound—

. . .

and then? Lightning in vain
can change you into something rich
and strange. Your mark was different.

•   •   •

What are you waiting for? The squirrel
beats his torch-tail on the pine tree's bark.
The half-moon with its peak sinks down
into the sun that swallows it. Day's done.

The sluggish mist gets startled by a gust,
but stands firm where it covers you.
Nothing ends, or everything,
if, brightness, you desert your cloud.

•   •   •

The spirit that dispenses
furlana and rigadoon at each new
season of the street
feeds on closet passion, finds it
more intense at every turn.

Your voice is this diffusing sense.
By wire, by wing, or wind, or chance,
favored by muse or machine, it echoes,
happy, sad. I'm saying something else
to one who doesn't know you, and
the theme is there insisting, *do re la sol sol* . . .

• • •

I free your forehead of the icicles
you gathered traveling the icy heights;
your wings were crushed by cyclones,
you startle awake.

Noon: in the square the medlar's black
shadow lengthens, a chilled sun stays on
in the sky; and the other shadows turning
into the alley don't know that you're here.

• • •

The gondola that slithers
through an acid tar-and-poppy glare,
the underhanded song that rose
up out of piles of rope,
the high doors shut on you, and merriment
from masks that were fleeing in droves—

one evening in a thousand, and my night
is darker. Down below
a blurred knot writhes, arousing me
by fits and starts, that makes me brother to
the serious eel-fisher on the shore.

· · ·

Is it salt that strafes, or hail?
It breaks the bellflowers, uproots the verbena.
An underwater tolling nears,
as if aroused by you, and moves away.

Hell's player piano ups its ante
all alone and climbs
the icy spheres—to gleam like you
when you were Lakmé,
trilling the Bell Song.

· · ·

At first light, when
a certain railroad
rumble speaks to me
of men in transit
locked in rock
tunnels lit by cuts of mottled
sky and water;

at first dark, when
the chisel etching at
the desk accelerates
its fervor and
the watchman nears:
light and dark, still human intervals
as long as you still knit them with your thread.

· · ·

The flower that repeats
forget me not
from the rim of the ravine
has no colors happier or purer
than the space passed between me and you.

A creaking starts up, pulling us apart,
the overweening blue won't reappear.
In haze you almost see, the cable car
takes me back where it's already dark.

· · ·

The frog, first to strike his chord
out of the pond that clogs with clouds
and rushes, the bent carobs' rustle
where a heatless sun puts out its torches,
late buzz of coleopters in the flowers
still sucking lymph, last noises, avaricious
country life. The hour ends at a gust:
a blackboard sky prepares
for famished horses to break out,
for sparks from their hooves.

· · ·

Shears, don't cut away that face
left lonely in my thinning memory,
don't turn her great listening look
into my usual haze.

A chill descends . . . The hard blow falls.
And on its own the struck acacia
shakes off the cicada's husk
into the first November mud.

· · ·

The reed that softly
molts its red
flabellum in spring;
the path in the ditch along the black
rivulet alive with dragonflies;
and the panting dog that trudges home,
his booty in his teeth, today

it's not for me to recognize;
but there where the reflection bakes
hottest and the cloud hangs low,
beyond her distant pupils, now
two simple light beams crossing.

And time passing.

. . .

. . . but so be it. Blare of a cornet
parleys with the swarms among the oaks.
In the seashell mirroring the sunset
a painted volcano brightly smokes.

The coin locked in the lava paperweight
shines too on the table, holding down
a sheaf of pages. Life, which seemed immense,
is smaller than your handkerchief.

Translated by Jonathan Galassi

Fueron abatidos cinco extremistas

Fuerzas de Seguridad atacaron con arm largas, morteros y bazookas una casa San Isidro. Otros 3 en S. M. de Tucumán

Una vista de la vivienda tomada por las Fuerzas de Seguridad, en la que pueden observarse los rastros del intenso ataque descargado el inmueble con diversas bocas de fuego.

BUENOS AIRES (NA). — Verdadera batalla, en El comunicado difundido por el Ejército en horas de la tarde de la víspera se ... mente. ... ca y Asunción. "Sobre ese lugar se realizó a acción y se intimó a los ... pantes del edificio a su ... quienes no acata ... abrieron el ... ores contra ... eas ... interinos ... namente a fin de ev ... personajes o a las rea ... reunas. Cinco muertos "Producto de la acción ... comunicado ... del edific ...

PERSONA DESAPARECIDA: N.CARLOTTO-Niño nacido durante el cautiverio de su madre Laura Estela Carlotto.

RELATO DE LOS HECHOS:

LAURA ESTELA CARLOTTO; 23 años, estudiante de Historia de la Universidad Nacional de La Plata; DNI n 11.614.026, fue secuestrada el 26 de noviembre de 1977 en la Capital Federal. Luego los padres de la misma tuvieron noticias de su cautiverio en varias oportunidades.

Laura Estela estaba embarazada de dos meses y medio al ser secuestrada. En abril de 1978 una persona llegó a la fábrica del padre señor Guido Carlotto y le manifestó que Laura Estela se encontraba bien, que esperaba su bebé para junio y que de ser varón le llamaría Guido como su padre, que para esa fecha estuvieran atentos a la casa cuna.

El 25 de agosto de 1978, los padres recibieron en su domicilio una citación de la comisaría 9 de La Plata, manifestándoles que deberían concurrir u

"My Mother Will Never Forgive Them"

—Laura Estela Carlotto, to a cellmate, August 25, 1978, as her two-month-old son, Guido, was taken from her and she was led away to be shot

Buenos Aires, June 1984

Matilde

A small, gray-haired man stood up in the back of the packed auditorium. "Tell me, doctor," he said. "How long does it take for the bones of a six-month-old child to dissolve?" I was sure I'd misunderstood. I'd been in Argentina less than twenty-four hours and hadn't spoken Spanish since I'd lived in Chile eleven years before. An Argentine medical student translated, and the forensic anthropologist Clyde Snow explained carefully that bones do not dissolve, "even" those of a six-month-old child. Tears came to the man's eyes. "Then Matilde is still alive," he said.

In September 1976, Mr. Miranda and his wife had opened their morning newspaper to see a photograph of their daughter and son-in-law's house pocked with bullet holes. The accompanying article described in detail how, the previous night, the police had engaged in an extended battle, involving bazookas and grenades, with five extremists at the house, who were ultimately killed by gunfire.

In January 1984, a month after the fall of the Argentine military government, the Mirandas were able to identify the

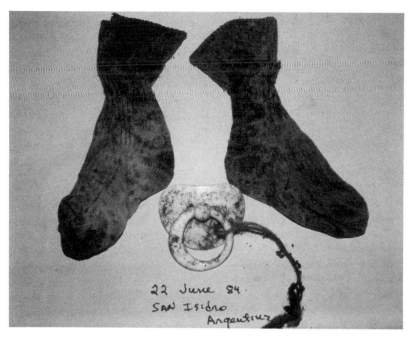

Fig. 1

extremists from burial certificates of the public cemetery in San Isidro. Two of the extremists were their son-in-law, Robert Francis Lanuscou, and their daughter, Barbara Miranda. The third extremist was their six-year-old granddaughter, Barbara; the fourth, their five-year-old grandson, Robert. The fifth extremist was identified only as "NN" (*ningun nombre*, no name) on the burial certificate, which also indicated her sex as female, her age as six months, and her cause of death as a bullet wound to the head. The bodies were exhumed; the bones of two adults and two approximately six-year-old children were lying side by side. But instead of a fifth set of bones, there was a little sleeper, a pacifier, and socks (*fig. 1*). Mrs. Miranda had given the sleeper to her six-month-old granddaughter Matilde eight years before. The cemetery director—who had held his job throughout the military period and now appeared somewhat uncomfortable— said brusquely that they shouldn't expect to find an infant's bones after so many years, that an infant's bones would dissolve. Mr. Miranda suspected otherwise.

Grandmothers

In 1975 a military junta seized power in Argentina, with the avowed purpose of saving the country from communism. They were explicit in their intentions:

> First we will kill all the subversives; then we will kill their collaborators; then . . . their sympathizers; then . . . . those who remain indifferent; and finally we will kill the timid.
> —General Iberico Saint Jean
> Governor of Buenos Aires Province, May 1976

A teaching slide from a counterterrorism course for Argentine military officers portrayed the subversives to whom the general referred. The branches of the Tree of Subversion *(fig. 2)* included leftists like the Popular Revolutionary Army (ERP) and Monteneros alongside Christian democrats, professors, journalists, and so on. The tree's roots were Marxism, Zionism, and Freemasonry.

The military was effective: people disappeared. Between 1975 and 1983, bodies of the disappeared reappeared in morgues, in unmarked graves, along riverbanks, and on ocean beaches. Among the disappeared were parents of small children and young pregnant women. Children old enough to talk were generally killed with their parents, as the two older Lanuscou children had been. However, bodies of infants did not appear. Infants simply vanished.

In 1977 the grandmothers of these children formed a human-rights group, the Grandmothers of the Plaza de Mayo, to demand information about their kidnapped children and grandchildren. They did this by marching every Thursday morning around the Plaza de Mayo in downtown Buenos Aires in front of the president's house, wearing white scarves and carrying pictures of their children and grandchildren *(fig. 3)*. A number of them were killed for this activity. But they continued to march.

As the years went on, anecdotal evidence accumulated that kidnapped grandchildren were still alive. Apparently, when young adults were seized by the military or the police and taken to torture centers, their small children would be taken to detention centers, then removed by people in authority. The men who removed these infants were often known, so

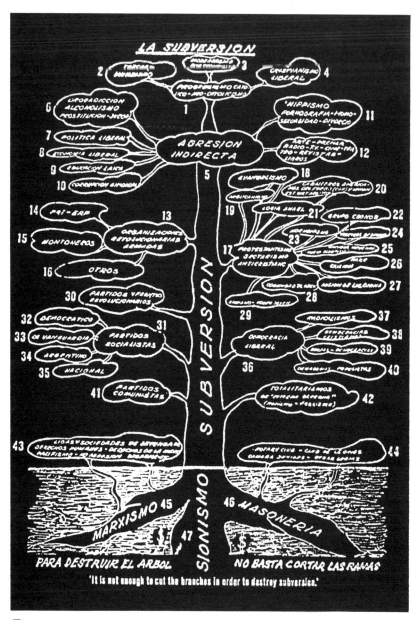

Fig. 2

Fig. 3

word would spread among the prisoners: this child was last seen with Father So-and-so, this one with Lieutenant So-and-so. Occasionally prisoners were released; they reported what they had heard to the Grandmothers.

If a young woman was pregnant when she was seized, she was usually kept alive (although tortured) until she was ready to give birth. There were no personnel at the military facilities to handle obstetrics, so an obstetrician or midwife would be kidnapped off the street. This became something of an occupational hazard for obstetricians and midwives and was more or less expected from time to time. The physician or midwife would be blindfolded and taken to a room where the young woman who had been tortured for several months would be lying on a bed in labor. The physician or midwife would be instructed not to speak to the woman and to deliver the child alive. In the vast majority of cases, the infants were delivered alive and well. Of course, in the course of hours of labor, words were exchanged, despite the presence of guards, and young mothers were able to whisper who they were. After the birth, the obstetrician or midwife would be blindfolded again, taken from the hospital, and dropped off somewhere in town. Most informed the Grandmothers of what had happened. At least one midwife was kidnapped and murdered for passing this information. The young mothers were taken away and shot. Their children apparently vanished.

But time passed. Between 1975 and 1983, children began to appear throughout Argentina in households where children weren't expected. For example, a child might appear in the household of a childless military or Mafia couple. The neighbors would be told that the wife had given birth; in several cases, neighbors knew that the wives had had hysterectomies years before. People in the neighborhood would quietly tell the Grandmothers about these unexplained children.

When the kidnapped children grew old enough to enter kindergarten, birth certificates had to be presented for school registration. Throughout Argentina, birth certificates that were clearly fraudulent began to appear. A certificate might say that a child had been born at home with no medical personnel in attendance, a virtually unheard-of occurrence among the middle-class military and police. Instead of a physician's signature above a typed name, there would appear an unintelligible scrawl or, in a few instances, the signature of a military physician who had access to birth certificates but nothing to do with obstetrics. Children with these birth certificates would be admitted to kindergarten. Then school secretaries would quietly call the Grandmothers.

Between 1977 and 1983, the Grandmothers accumulated anecdotal information. They filled hundreds of black binders. They sought out witnesses, organized data, followed military officers they suspected of holding their grandchildren, developed hypotheses, and marched.

In 1983 the military was forced to withdraw from power following their defeat in the Malvinas/Falklands war. Elections were held, and the human-rights lawyer Raoul Alfonsin was elected president. Alfonsin's first act was to create the Commission on the Disappearance of Persons to determine what had happened to victims of kidnapping during the eight years of military dictatorship. Thousands of people were interviewed. The Grandmothers and other human-rights groups were able to provide additional information. By June 1984, details had been collected for 8,970 persons; relatives and friends of the others were afraid to come forward. Based on careful measurements of underreporting in sample areas of the country, best estimates are that approximately fifteen thousand persons disappeared. The list included 145 children who had been kidnapped with their parents or born in captivity. The list grew to include 210 children over the next few years as more families spoke out.

The Commission on the Disappearance of Persons asked for technical assistance in identifying the remains being exhumed. The Grandmothers asked for technical assistance in identifying living children as they were located in the households of suspected kidnappers. So in June 1984 five Americans went to Buenos Aires, where we found ourselves discussing forensics and genetics with an audience of judges, human-rights workers, and families of the disappeared on one side of the hall, and military and police on the other. Seats in the middle were mostly unoccupied.

Genes

By 1984 the Grandmothers thought they knew who many of their grandchildren were, and where and with whom they were living. But as they told me, their evidence was circumstantial. They needed to be able to *prove* who their children were. They needed genetics.

Immediately after the first meeting, where I encountered Matilde's grandfather, the Grandmothers took me to their office. The office is a converted middle-class apartment in the center of Buenos Aires. Its former living room and bedrooms are lined with black binders, and one bedroom has been converted into a computer room. There is also a kitchen, which was a blessing, since we lived for eighteen-hour days on Grandmotherly sandwiches and tea stronger than an American could have imagined. On the living-room wall are hundreds of photographs of disappeared children and grandchildren *(fig. 4)*.

The Grandmothers immediately posed the practical question: If we locate a child whose identity is unknown, but whom we believe to be the child of disappeared parents and the grand-child of known grandparents, can we determine whether the child is or is not actually related to those grandparents? They also pointed out that they would not be satisfied with proving who a child was *not*, that is, that he was not in fact the biological child of a military couple claiming to be his parents. That would be easier to do. One could apply for a court order to test the child against the alleged parents. But that would not be enough: it was necessary to prove *who* a child was, not only that he was one of the kidnap victims.

We drew a hypothetical family tree comprising four living grandparents, the deceased parents, and a child who might or might not be related to them. I asked the Grandmothers if we could obtain a small amount of blood from each grandparent and the child. "The grandparents would be easy," they said, "and we could request a court order to sample the child." So I explained that we could type each grandparent and the child for each of several genes. A child will have two copies (called alleles) of each gene, one inherited from his mother and the other from

Fig. 4

his father. Each parent, in turn, has inherited one allele from the grandmother and one from the grandfather. Thus, for every gene, a child's alleles will be copies of alleles of his grandparents. If the child's alleles of a certain gene failed to match those of any of the grandparents, we would know immediately that he was not a member of this family. However, if, for each gene, the child shared one allele with a maternal grandparent and the other allele with a paternal grandparent, he *might* be related to the family. For any gene, we could calculate the odds that the match indicated a biological relationship rather than occurring by chance. For example, typing ABO blood groups would not tell us very much. A child and two grandparents might be blood group O. But so is half the population of Argentina. Blood group O would not establish a child's identity.

What we needed were genes that had many different alleles in the population of Argentina, so that the appearance of the same alleles in a child and two grandparents was very likely to reflect relationship rather than a coincidental match. In 1984 the most varied human genes known were the HLA genes, which code for the histocompatibility antigens that must match for tissue transplants. The HLA genes would certainly be informative enough to resolve many cases. However, in 1984, HLA typing was subject to severe practical limitations: it could only be done on fresh blood and required highly specific reagents. Before leaving California for Buenos Aires, I had come to the tentative but frustrating conclusion that the Grandmothers' identification project, while theoretically straightforward, was going to be impossible in practice: shipping hundreds of blood samples from all over Argentina to the United States within hours of their being drawn would be a logistical nightmare, yet there would be no lab in Argentina capable of HLA typing at the scene.

I needn't have worried. The Grandmothers had already identified a laboratory at the Durand Hospital in Buenos Aires that was well equipped and fully competent in the clinical typing of HLA. So we immediately began to work with Ana Maria DiLonardo, the laboratory director, and carried out virtually all the HLA typing there for the first cases.

Fig. 5

Paula

In 1978, when Paula Logares *(fig. 5)* was twenty-two months old, she and her parents, Claudio Logares and Monica Greenspan, were kidnapped. Claudio and Monica have not been seen again, nor have their bodies been recovered. Five years later, a child—who appeared closer to age seven than to age five—was registered in a kindergarten as Paula Lavallen. Ruben Lavallen had been a guard at the detention center to which Paula Logares's parents were taken. He was known by people who had been released from that detention center to have been a particularly brutal torturer. He had also been seen leaving the detention center in May 1978 with a small child. The Grandmothers learned about the kindergarten registration in 1983.

Immediately after the fall of the military regime, the Grandmothers obtained a court order to take a blood sample from Paula Lavallen. We also obtained blood samples from Monica's brothers, sister, and mother, and from Claudio's mother and father. Everyone's blood was typed for HLA (as well as blood groups such as ABO, Rh, and MNS) at the Durand

Hospital. Monica's father had died of a stroke shortly after the kidnapping of his daughter and granddaughter. However, we could reconstruct his genetic types from his surviving children (Monica's brothers and sister)—without using the information from Paula, of course.

Of Paula's two HLA types, one matched Claudio's father; the other matched one of Monica's brothers, her sister, and their father. It was clear that Paula could be a member of this family, having inherited one HLA type from her Greenspan grandfather and the other from her Logares grandfather. The conclusive evidence came from the fact that each HLA type is rare. The probability that a child with Paula's types would match the Logares-Greenspan family by chance was less than one in one thousand; the likelihood that Paula was indeed a member of the family was 99.9 percent.

The Grandmothers presented this information to the court. The judge declared that because Ruben Lavallen and his wife claimed Paula was their biological child, they had a right to be tested to determine whether they and Paula also matched. Lavallen refused, claiming testing would be an invasion of their privacy. But Ruben Lavallen stopped claiming that Paula was their biological child.

The judge accepted the evidence that Paula was the kidnapped grandchild of the Logares and Greenspan families and was prepared to restore her to her grandparents. However, the case was immediately appealed. Lavallen claimed that his family was the only family Paula remembered, that to remove her from his household would be far more traumatic than to allow her to continue to stay with him, and that he had not harmed Paula. The appellate court judge accepted this argument and reversed the previous court decision.

In November 1984 the Grandmothers took Paula's case to the Supreme Court of Argentina. They made five points. First, it is unclear what a person remembers from before the age of twenty-two months. It was true that Paula had not talked about the kidnapping, but there were possible explanations (including the likely involvement of Lavallen in the kidnapping) other than not remembering. Second, the man with whom Paula was living and who was acting as her father was very likely to have been directly involved in the murder of her true mother and father. Third, the murder of Claudio and Monica, and of thousands of others, was no longer secret. Paula would eventually learn the truth. To learn as a young adult that she had been raised by the murderer of her parents would be far more traumatic than being told the truth right away. Fourth, kidnapping is not adoption. Kidnapping is a crime, and remains a crime even if society takes six years to solve it. And finally, to fail to prosecute crimes against children if the child in an individual case was not harmed is to grant invulnerability to criminals who prey on children. For the sake of children everywhere, whether victims of the Argentine military government or of an isolated criminal attack, it was essential that adults be held responsible for these crimes.

In December 1984 the Supreme Court ordered that Paula be returned to her grandparents. When Paula went home with Monica Greenspan's mother, Elsa, she walked into the house she had not seen since she was twenty-two months old, turned left to the bedroom she used to sleep in, opened the door, looked at the bed, and asked, "Where is my teddy bear?"

Knitting

Late one night during my first week with the Grandmothers, when I was stretching my memory and my Spanish to their limits in my effort to absorb everything, I turned to the Grandmother who was showing me a photograph of a detention center wall where the names of babies were written in blood, and I told this Grandmother that she reminded me of Madame Defarge. She looked at me with a puzzled expression and asked, "Who is Madame Defarge?" (Argentinians and Americans don't necessarily read the same books in high school.) So I explained how Madame Defarge had spent the years before the French Revolution knitting into scarves the names of those who had imprisoned and killed people and against whom the people would strike later. The Grandmother smiled and said, "My dear girl, I don't have time to knit anymore; now I use a personal computer."

To me, this remark will always represent the Grandmothers. This Grandmother was sixty-eight years old. She had a right to be home knitting for her grandchildren, but she no longer had a grandchild. She no longer had a son. Life had been very unfair to her; her response was to learn to use a personal computer.

Tatiana and Laura

Not all children were found in the hands of military or police or their collaborators. Of the fifty children whom the Grandmothers have found, six had been adopted in completely good faith by families who had nothing to do with the military. Two of these, Tatiana and Laura, were adopted by the S—— family. When the S—— family applied to be adoptive parents in 1977, a military-appointed judge offered them two sisters, a four-year-old and an infant, whom he claimed had been abandoned by their mother. Mr. and Mrs. S—— were skeptical that any mother would give up two little girls but were repeatedly reassured that the children had been deserted. They adopted the girls. Soon Tatiana began to describe how her mother and father had been taken away in the trunk of a gray car. (The police used gray Ford Falcons to transport their victims.)

In 1980, at the height of the military dictatorship, Mrs. S—— was in downtown Buenos Aires the morning of a Grandmothers' march around the Plaza de Mayo. In the hands of one of the Grandmothers, she saw a poster of Tatiana and Laura. She walked across the Plaza past the machine-gun-carrying guards, touched the Grandmother on the sleeve, and said, "I think I have your children."

Tatiana's and Laura's identities were no longer in doubt, nor was their future. The girls remain with the S—— family. They have been told the truth about their biological family, have taken back their own names, and visit their grandparents, aunts, uncles, and cousins. They are very much aware that they were not abandoned and that they are loved by both their adoptive and their biological relatives.

Buenos Aires, September 1987

Maria José

In July 1977 Heidi Lemos, her daughter, Monica Lemos, and her son-in-law, Gustavo Lavalle, were all kidnapped. Monica and Gustavo's three-year-old daughter was visiting a friend and escaped. Gustavo died under torture within days. Monica was eight months pregnant; she was kept alive until she gave birth, then she was killed and her newborn daughter Maria José taken. Heidi was imprisoned and tortured for seven months, then released.

Heidi quickly found her elder granddaughter. Ten years later, she and the Grandmothers located Maria José in the household of a woman who had been in charge of pregnant prisoners at the detention center. HLA and blood groups were sufficient to identify Maria José, and she was returned to Heidi by order of the Federal Court of San Martin in September 1987.

The case of Maria José Lavalle Lemos revealed to us an obvious but important truth: genetics was powerful, but in this case we had also been very lucky. Maria José's only surviving grandparent was Heidi Lemos, her maternal grandmother. Gustavo had no surviving relatives and Monica no brothers or sisters. But Heidi's undisputed first granddaughter was alive, so the genotypes of the two of them provided enough genetic information to obtain a probability greater than 99 percent that Maria José was a member of the Lavalle Lemos family. But this immediately raised the question of what to do with a family with few living relatives.

Furthermore, by 1987 our success in identifying children had brought with it new questions. In 1986 the Argentine parliament passed a law establishing a voluntary National Genetic Data Bank. This law specified that anyone who had lost a relative during the military dictatorship could have a genetic pedigree constructed for their family and DNA samples collected to be tested against kidnapped children who came to light in the future.

This law was a tremendous boon to the Grandmothers, but in practice it meant that each child was now to be tested against a large number of families. In the past, we had tested only specific hypotheses, based on the Grandmothers' circumstantial but generally highly reliable evidence. If two hundred families were to be screened, it was possible we might have an HLA match purely by chance. We had to avoid, at all costs, falsely identifying a child with a family: every identity had to be genuine. With a panel of two hundred families, the chances of a coincidental match were greatly increased. We would need more genetic information.

Thus we had two new scientific problems to solve. Many families were likely to have only one or a few relatives alive, and we now had a large number of families against which to test newly found children. So what was to be done?

I was stewing over this in the Grandmothers' office. The Grandmothers, in their typical fashion, hugged me and gave me a strong cup of tea. "Go back to Berkeley, dear," one of them said, "and give us a call in a couple of weeks when you've figured it out."

Berkeley, 1987–88

Mitochondrial DNA

So I went back to Berkeley and into the office of Allan Wilson, my Ph.D. advisor from twenty years before. Allan Wilson was known to us as "the Father of Eve." This somewhat whimsical nickname grew out of his enchantment with mitochondrial DNA. Mitochondrial DNA is the ideal molecule for the Grandmothers' work.

What is mitochondrial DNA, and why is it so useful? Mitochondrial DNA is found in the cytoplasm of each cell, not in the nucleus. In particular, mitochondria are found in very large numbers in ova, but only in the tail of the sperm and do not enter the fertilized egg. This means that every child inherits mitochondrial DNA only from his mother, never from his father. Thus a child will have the same mitochondrial DNA type as his brothers and sisters, his mother, his maternal aunts and uncles, his maternal grandmother, his maternal grandmother's siblings,

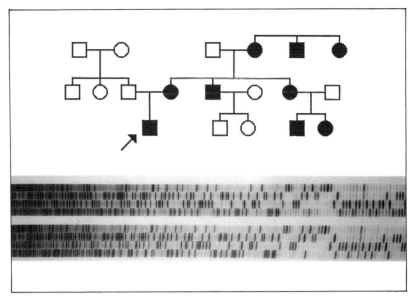

Fig. 6

his first cousins through maternal aunts, and so on *(fig. 6, top)*. For the purposes of the Grandmothers, this meant that any of these purely maternal relatives would have mitochondrial DNA identical to that of a kidnapped child.

However, mitochondrial DNA identity within a maternal lineage would only be useful for identifying a child if maternal lineages were distinguishable from one another. That is, there must be genetic variation across different maternal lineages. As it happens, one part of the mitochondrial DNA sequence is the most variable region of the human genome. There is enough genetic variation in this twelve-hundred-basepair sequence to distinguish between one maternal lineage and another. Probably the reason that this region of mitochondrial DNA is so variable among humans is that it does not code for any genes, so there has been no selective pressure during human evolution to retain any particular sequence. This variation underlies the fascination mitochondrial DNA held for Allan Wilson and other molecular geneticists interested in evolution.

Identification by mitochondrial DNA was made feasible by a technique called PCR, the polymerase chain reaction. Between

1984 and 1987, genetics underwent a revolution. One part of that revolution was the development of PCR technology, which allows one to obtain, even from a very small sample of blood, enough DNA to determine an entire genetic sequence *(fig. 6, bottom)*. Allan's lab had already exploited PCR for mitochondrial DNA studies and had worked out quick and reliable methods for directly sequencing the DNA product.

So mitochondrial DNA presented the unbeatable convergence of three pieces of biology and technology: a purely maternal molecule, so that any maternal relative could substitute for any other maternal relative; extraordinary levels of genetic variation; and simple direct sequencing.

Buenos Aires, 1988

Maria Cristina, Martin, Valeria, and Ricardo

In May 1977, Valeria Belaustegui and her husband, Ricardo Waisberg, were kidnapped. In July 1977, her brother, Martin Belaustegui, and his wife, Maria Cristina Lopez Guerra, were seized. Valeria and Martin's older brother was also seized. Valeria and Maria Cristina were in the first trimester of pregnancies when they were abducted. None of the five adults has reappeared, nor have their bodies been recovered. The Grandmothers heard that Valeria and Maria Cristina had been kept alive until they gave birth and then murdered.

In 1988, ten years after the births would have occurred, a ten-year-old boy (whom we'll call Alejandro) was brought to the attention of the Grandmothers. The woman who introduced Alejandro to the Grandmothers had cared for him since 1978, when he was given to her as a present by her then-companion, who had close ties to the military. She reported that she had been terrified to tell anyone about the incident until her former companion was arrested in 1988 by the civilian government (on criminal charges apparently unrelated to the child). She came forward because she believed Alejandro had a right to know his identity and his surviving relatives. By complete coincidence, Alejandro was a student at the same school that all five of the murdered young adults had attended as children. Based on Alejandro's age, the Grandmothers believed he might be the child of one of the young women in this family. We were asked to test this by DNA sequencing.

We received blood samples from Matilde Herrera, the mother of Valeria and Martin Belaustegui; from Ebe Lopez Guerra, the mother of Maria Cristina Lopez Guerra; and from Alejandro. If Alejandro were the child of Valeria and Ricardo, Matilde Herrera would be his maternal grandmother and their mitochondrial DNA sequences should match. If Alejandro were the child of Maria Cristina and Martin, Ebe Lopez Guerra would be his maternal grandmother and *their* mitochondrial sequences should match.

Alejandro does not match either Matilde or Ebe. We analyzed four hundred basepairs of mitochondrial DNA and found that he differed from Matilde at three sites and from Ebe at eight. Alejandro is not a grandchild in this family. The Grandmothers are still attempting to determine his identity.

Berkeley, January 1992

The Grandmothers continue to collect blood samples from hundreds of surviving relatives searching for kidnapped children. Last week, samples from twenty-one relatives arrived; we expect thirty-two more next week. My sixteen-year-old daughter, Emily, whose Spanish is much better than mine, read through the documentation accompanying this week's shipment. "Three more children have asked the Grandmothers for help," she said. "They've listed the families who are the most likely candidates for each child, but they want you to cross-check all the families against these three and the other unknown children." Emily grinned. "Of course, they want your results *lo mas pronto posible.*"

Of the 210 children known to have been kidnapped at birth or in infancy, 50 (including Paula, Tatiana, Laura, and Maria José) have been identified, 12 (including Alejandro) have been found but have not been matched with a family, and 148 (including Guido Carlotto and Matilde Lanuscou) are still missing. Meanwhile, the government in Argentina has become much more hostile to the Grandmothers' efforts than it was under the Alfonsin presidency of 1984–89. In particular, it is increasingly difficult to work within the Argentine judicial system. However, the Grandmothers remain undaunted. They point out that most of the kidnapped children are now at least sixteen years old. Very soon these children will have the legal right to determine their identities for themselves. For this purpose, DNA sequences will be available to them. Even though the grandparents of a kidnapping victim may die before the grandchild is found, the young adult's maternal lineage will be identifiable using the genetic information the Grandmothers leave behind. A young person can then be put in touch with his family and his history.

For the past fifteen years, the Grandmothers have been searching for their kidnapped grandchildren. Now these grandchildren are looking for them.

•   •   •

. . .
And finally
when
the day
comes when they ask you
to identify the body
and you see me
and a voice says
we killed him
the poor bastard died
he's dead
when they tell you
that I am
completely absolutely definitely
dead
don't believe them
don't believe them
don't believe them.

—Ariel Dorfman, "Last Will and Testament"

A Pulse

Find the place
in silence
that is a person

or like a person
or like not
needing a person.

.

After the heart attack
she fills her apartment
with designer accents—

piece by piece.

.

This is a bed,
an abiding
at least,

close to *lastly*
but nicer.

.

Light changes:

Separation
anxiety refers
to this

as next
tears itself off.

·

A hospital calendar
shows the sun going down
on an old-time,
round, lime-green
diner.

·

Just a quick trip back
to mark the spot
where things stop
looking familiar.

from *Trilce*

XXXII

999 calorías.
Rumbbb . . . . Trrraprrrr rrach . . . chaz
Serpentínica u del bizcochero
enjirafada al tímpano.

Quién como los hielos. Pero nó.
Quién como lo que va ni más ni menos.
Quién como el justo medio.

1,000 calorías.
Azulea y ríe su gran cachaza
el firmamento gringo. Baja
el sol empavado y le alborota los cascos
al más frío.

Remeda al cuco: Rooooooeeeis . . . . . .
tierno autocarril, móvil de sed,
que corre hasta la playa.

Aire, aire! Hielo!
Si al menos el calor(—Mejor
              no digo nada.

Y hasta la misma pluma
con que escribo por último se troncha.

Treinta y tres trillones trescientos treinta
y tres calorías.

• • •

XXXII

999 calories.
Roombbb . . . . Hulllablll llust . . . ster
Serpenteenic e of the sweet roll vendor
girafeted to the eardrum.

Lucky the ices. But no.
Lucky that which goes neither more nor less.
Lucky the golden mean.

1000 calories.
The gringo firmament looks blue
and chuckles up its hocker. The razzed
sun sets and scrambles the skulls
even of the coldest.

It talks cuckootalk: Weeeeeetrozzz . . . . . .
the tender rail car, rolling from thirst,
that runs up to the beach.

Air, air! Ice!
If at least the calor(—Better
              I say nothing.

And even the very pen
with which I write finally cracks up.

Thirty-three trillion three hundred and thirty-
three calories.

· · ·

XXXVI

Pugnamos ensartarnos por un ojo de aguja,
enfrentados, a las ganadas.
Amoniácase casi el cuarto ángulo del círculo.
¡Hembra se continúa el macho, a raiz
de probables senos, y precisamente
a raiz de cuanto no florece!

¿Por ahí estás, Venus de Milo?
Tú manqueas apenas, pululando
entrañada en los brazos plenarios
de la existencia,
de esta existencia que todaviiza
perenne imperfección.
Venus de Milo, cuyo cercenado, increado
brazo revuélvese y trata de encodarse
a través de verdeantes guijarros gagos,
ortivos nautilos, aunes que gatean
recién, vísperas inmortales.
Laceadora de inminencias, laceadora
del paréntesis.

Rehusad, y vosotros, a posar las plantas
en la seguridad dupla de la Armonía.
Rehusad la simetría a buen seguro.
Intervenid en el conflicto
de puntas que se disputan
en la más torionda de las justas
el salto por el ojo de la aguja!

Tal siento ahora al meñique
demás en la siniestra. Lo veo y creo
no debe serme, o por lo menos que está
en sitio donde no debe.

XXXVI

We struggle to thread ourselves through a needle's eye,
face to face, hellbent on winning.
The fourth angle of the circle ammoniafies almost.
Female is continued the male, on the basis
of probable breasts, and precisely
on the basis of how much does not flower!

Are you that way, Venus de Milo?
You hardly act crippled, pullulating
enwombed in the plenary arms
of existence,
of this existence that neverthelessez
perpetual imperfection.
Venus de Milo, whose cut-off, increate
arm swings round and tries to elbow
across greening stuttering pebbles,
ortive nautili, recently crawling
evens, immortal on the eves of.
Lassoer of imminences, lassoer
of the parenthesis.

Refuse, all of you, to set foot
on the double security of Harmony.
Truly refuse symmetry.
Intervene in the conflict
of points that contend
in the most rutty of jousts
for the leap through the needle's eye!

So now I feel my little finger
moreover on my left. I see it and think
it shouldn't be me, or at least that it's
in a place where it shouldn't.

Y me inspira rabia y me azarea
y no hay cómo salir de él, sino haciendo
la cuenta de que hoy es jueves.

¡Ceded al nuevo impar
                    potente de orfandad!

•   •   •

XXXVIII

Este cristal aguarda ser sorbido
en bruto por boca venidera
sin dientes. No desdentada.
Este cristal es pan no venido todavía.

Hiere cuando lo fuerzan
y ya no tiene cariños animales.
Mas si se la apasiona, se melaría
y tomaría la horma de los sustantivos
que se adjetivan de brindarse.

Quienes lo ven allí triste individuo
incoloro, lo envirían por amor,
por pasado y a lo más por futuro:
si él no dase por ninguno de sus costados;
si él espera ser sorbido de golpe
y en cuanto transparencia, por boca venidera que ya no tendrá dientes.

Este cristal ha pasado de animal,
y márchase ahora a formar las izquierdas,
los nuevos Menos.
Déjenlo solo no más.

And it inspires me with rage and alarms me
and there is no way out of it, except by
pretending that today is Thursday.

Make way for the new odd number
                                    potent with orphanhood!

•   •   •

XXXVIII

This crystal waits to be sipped
in the rough by a future mouth
without teeth. Not toothless.
This crystal is bread yet to come.

It wounds when they force it
and no longer shows animal affection.
But if one excites it, it could honefy
and become the mold for substantives
which adjectivize in self-offerings.

Those who see it a sad colorless
individual, could dispatch it with love,
for the past and at most for the future:
if it does not surrender any of its sides;
if it waits to be sipped in a gulp
and once transparent, by a future mou-
that will no longer have teeth.

This crystal has passed from animal,
and now goes off to form lefts,
the new Minuses.
Just leave it alone.

Translated by Clayton Eshleman, with Julio Ortega

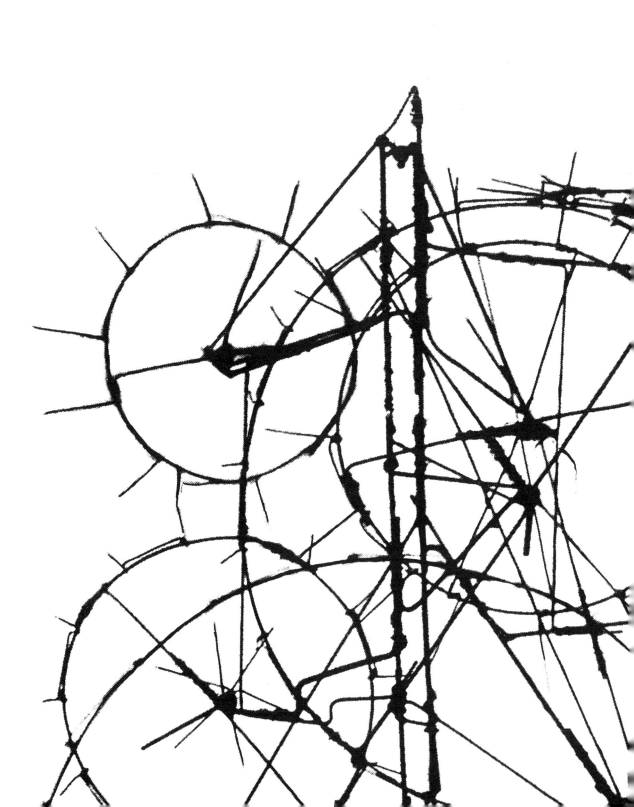

A
Magic
Stronger
Than
Death

Jean Tinguely
(1925–1991)

A year ago *Grand Street* was planning to collaborate with Jean Tinguely on a portfolio of new work. These plans had to be abandoned at Tinguely's death last September. Instead we offer this portfolio to honor one of the century's most energetic and inventive artists.

The works in the portfolio are drawn from what turned out to be the last exhibition in which Tinguely participated directly: the magnificent retrospective, "A Magic Stronger Than Death," staged by his close friend Pontus Hulten at the Palazzo Grassi, Venice (1987) and Centre Georges Pompidou, Musée National d'Art Moderne, Paris (1988–89). Our heartfelt thanks are given to Pontus Hulten, Jean-Yves Mock, and Niki de Saint Phalle, who each knew and worked with Jean Tinguely.

2.

3.

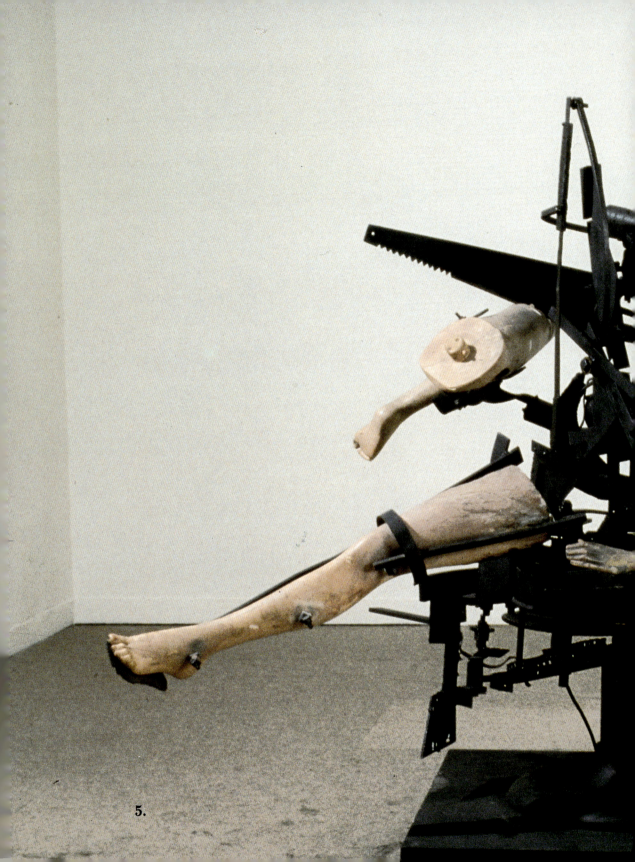

5.

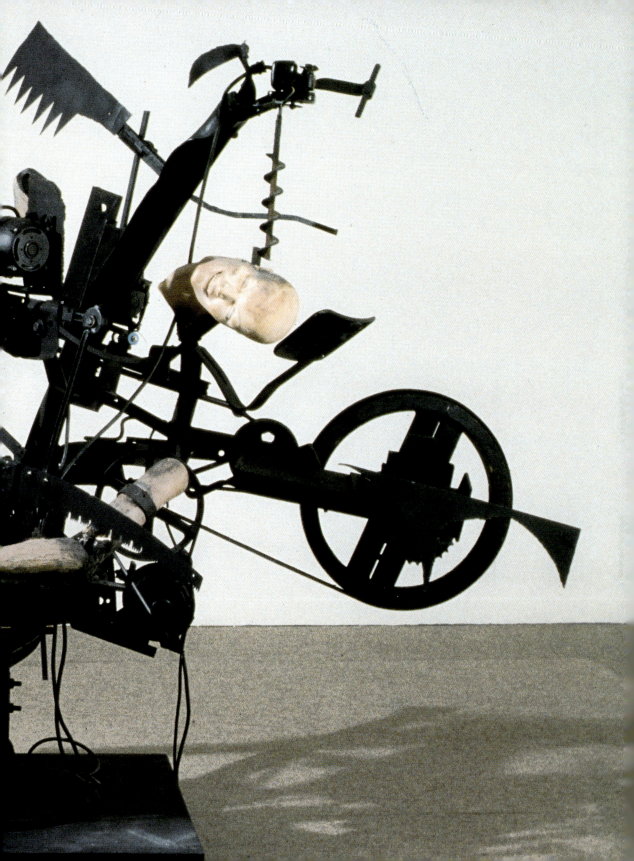

6.

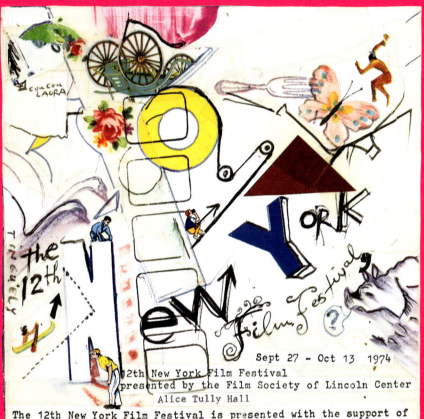

Sept 27 – Oct 13 1974

12th New York Film Festival
presented by the Film Society of Lincoln Center
Alice Tully Hall

The 12th New York Film Festival is presented with the support of
the New York State Council on the Arts

8.

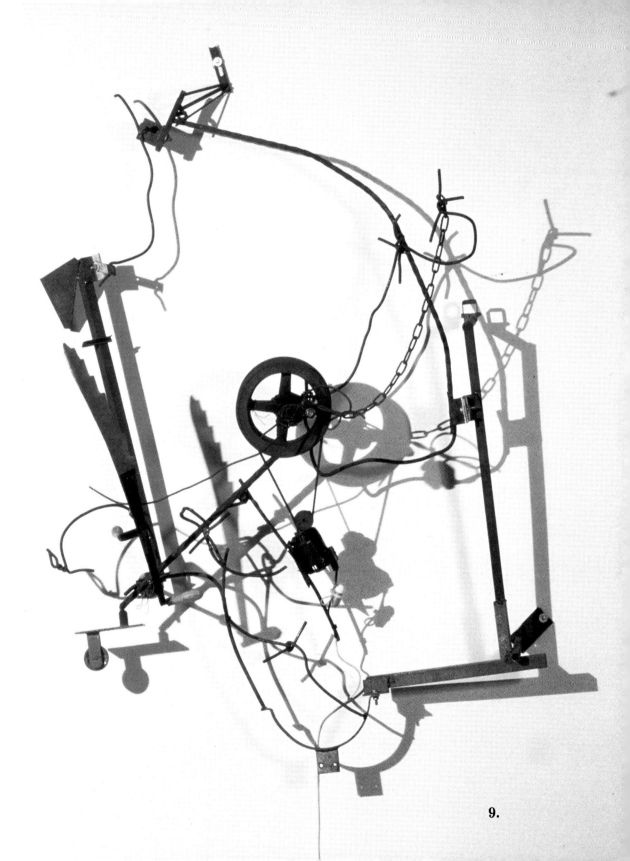

9.

10.

11.

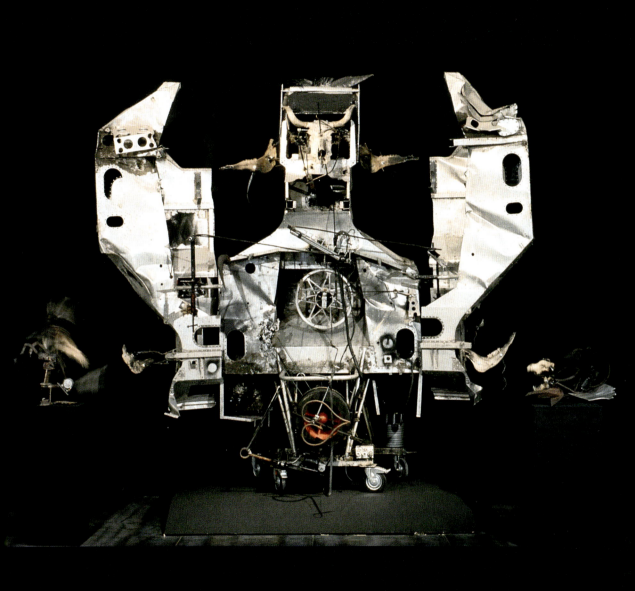

13.

14.

15.

A Magic Stronger Than Death

1. *Moulin à prière*, 1954 (detail)
   Motorized assemblage
   29⅛ x 21 x 14 in.
   Museum of Fine Arts, Houston

2. *Totem IV*, 1960
   Motorized assemblage
   57 x 18⅛ x 18⅛ in.
   Moderna Museet, Stockholm

3. *Bascule No. 1*, 1960
   Motorized assemblage
   26⅜ x 26⅜ x 22½ in.
   Private collection

4. *Motor-Cocktail*, 1965
   Motorized assemblage
   27⅛ x 19 x 15 in.
   Private collection
   (Printed in black/white reversal)

5. *Dissecting Machine*, 1965
   Motorized assemblage
   72¾ x 74 x 83¾ in.
   The Menil Collection, Houston

6. *Hommage rotative (La Plume
   furieuse)*, 1974 (detail)
   Motorized assemblage
   30⅜ x 29½ x 27½ in.
   Private collection

7. Poster maquette, for Richard
   Roud—12th New York Film
   Festival, 1974
   Drawing and collage
   6 x 6 in.
   Private collection

8. *Le Chien de Niki*, 1981
   Motorized assemblage
   22⅞ x 28⅜ x 15 in.
   Private collection

9. *Le Chevalier à la rose*, 1984
   Motorized assemblage
   94½ x 72⅞ x 23⅝ in.
   Private collection

10. *Les Sorcières* or *Blanche-Neige
    et les Sept Nains*, 1985
    Set of motorized assemblages
    c. 6 x 25 x 10 ft.
    Private collection
    (Installation view, Paris, 1989)

11. *L'Agression*, 1986
    Drawing
    17⅜ x 13½ in.
    Private collection

12. *Lola T. 180—Mémorial pour
    Joakim B.*, 1988
    Motorized assemblage
    118⅛ x 157½ x 59 in.
    Private collection

13. *Torino*, c. 1987
    Drawing on black paper
    19⅝ x 27½ in.
    Private collection

14. *Friedrich Engels*, 1988
    Motorized assemblage
    57 x 51⅛ x 63 in.
    Private collection

15. *Jean-Jacques Rousseau*, 1988
    Motorized assemblage
    67 x 59 x 51⅛ in.
    Private collection

The First Step

A journey of ten thousand li begins with the first step.

In the country of the middle
The person in the middle is king
No one walking on the outskirts
No sprechstimme singing in Beijing

Splash of water at the end of the ship
Flash of sky at the end of the plane
Dash of suit at the end of the man
Clash of music going away

There is no molding
There is no "souk"
There is no pounding and no landing
Nothing but Chinese absence soup

A journey of five hundred limits
Begins with the first one met
After the first, one knows that this is not
The "real" journey and yet and yet

No Africa, no rest of Asia, no Europe no sweet continent
No Italy no England no Portugal no Spain
And Spain exists outside the scientific revolution
As Sicily exists outside it, no Brazil, no Cuba, only China

One sensuous life and three parks
Two kinds of government eighteen minority nationalities
One woman two women a man three
A long corral of roofs a boat an evening

The new dawn rises
With the first ray of the sun
Why are you going away?
From the born smoke rises

The first whisper of departure starts in his nostrils
It starts there though it comes from far away
His life today is like a stereopticon
He sees more than at any other time

No chamber orchestra to say when you have arrived there
No religious chorus to say when you have gotten there
No French horn section to say when at last you are there
Only a beat de-tuck-tucking of a single heart

Seventeen intellectuals on a train
The train is not going nowhere
Inside it as it is going somewhere
The intellectuals' minds are moving around

Panda on a stamp
Hing Chow post office
Panda on a stage
Beijing Zoo

"Call Amalgamated Chinoiseries and get me the manager!
Give me a bowl of the share-holding poundings of the sea!
Let them be like flowrets on my army bandage!
I want to never leave the hinges of this diamond sleep!"

So much depends upon
The room temperature
Hitches up skirt. He lifts
Phonograph needle. Day fleets down

The basket of laundry starts on Huang Yin Street
It moves through the crowded city with a bustle of napkins
Finally it arrives at the large hotel
There it is undone like a flapping of wings

I have never
Seen such streets
Such had never
Sight of me

Man woman baby bicycle basket
Truck crossroad vanishing composite northern
Great Wall resolute slow
Table rock needle tire sting

With song of self-pity denigrated by taste
Soaring apathetic and night-canoey
Walking along streets that seem going to waste
Outside Paris and in Shanghai and Huan-Shi City

If only you had come
When the need was highest
Romantic hooey
But some drenched train

Green moss scabs the sides of trees
Wisteria-reaches clutch the wood railing of the porch
A diet is proposed: Don't eat.
The point of life is discussed: Sleep together.

The walls of this farmhouse
Are made of stone
Everyone thinks
To live a long time

In the post office
No postage meter
No automatic box to give stamps
No special delivery and no federal express

Showers fall down
Man is unhappy
Out comes the sun
Shakes off and smiles

He speaks crop language
To farm analysts
Beside the white
Unanalyzed chickens

Skeletons in Salvadorean pits
Black needles of Hong Kong
Ships burning like coats eagles like aprons
Gas the good air of paradise turned to stench

At the poultry market
The sun shines. A chicken jumps up
At the sea-bait market
A snail jumps up

These pink Chinese characters, San She Dan Chen Pills!
Two birds with blue back-feathers
Lean over a spray of blossoms white and pink
Take them for your health Signature baseball
Followed by the author's explanation

Post office has stamps yellow color green blue orange red brown
Many picture panda embrace follow plus leaders ruling men
Lick of stamp to other side come glue and postal paste fellow
Bring a lamp to mailbox show by light how get them in

No stopping those officials on the way to the airport
No reasoning with them to about-face
No saying Better to stop and have a good time
Good time for them is this not our good time

He was sorry to be so angry
He was sorry to be so nervous
He was sorry to be so absent
He was sorry to be so stunned

No soft breast
No soft bottom
No soft sleeper
No one on the train

After a mile
No more music
After five miles
No more news

While she was there
While he is here
Pink buds blossom
In the People's Park

The baby is not a soft sleeper but a hard sleeper
The train from Kunming to Shanghai the baby runs on alone

How amazing to see so many hundreds
Of international celebrities at once!
They are all in a picture on a poster
They stand pasted to a billboard—lucky ones

The automobile holds still
Inside is an Official
The automobile moves
The Official sits back and smiles

Only canal with muddy boat
Purple what-have-you
First mate smiling
Second or third face smiling

Perimeter of lake
People very busy
Only one loony-seeming man
Stands and screams before Authorities

Moment to hush those talkies
Very strange man
Feminine police mood filling cabinet
Very very strange man

In head no thought
On heart no scar
In mouth no word
Dead so far

The Shanghai skyscrapers shine like fire of dragons
The Huangpu River Bridge is like a palace woman's hairpin
The People's Park is like a jungle without trees or animals
The people crowded on the boat are like boxes in a store

No fish on menu
No meat on menu
No vegetable on menu
No rice no tea

The young day ruins itself for democracy
The blue river stabs itself into trees

No Beijing Opera
No King with red face
No King with white face
No Queen with whitish-blue face

Ivy falling forward
Over gray great wall
Men seeming lacking in compassion
Driving a human pile driver twenty miles long

She wakes up goes to market
A fine white hen flies to the floor
She tries to pick it up
But she does not have enough yuan

The soft sleeper leaves the city at dawn
The hard sleeper leaves at the same time
One sleeper is attached to the other sleeper
Rolling quietly they are the same train

Today in the dimness
Nine persons eating Dim Sum
Tonight in the darkness
Ninety-seven persons eating shark

No pigs standing in front of the grocery store
No wagon of cow manure stopped in the middle of the major road
No huge advertisements for doctors in the center of the square
No women tugging their husbands through canal pits thick with mud

No burning face from suddenly fired sexual excitement
No teacher with white hand turning away embarrassed and pleased
No warrior with grim expression keeping watch
No herbalist no pencils no camera salesman nothing four hundred city blocks

No banners signaling reprieve from someone's dying
No reverse funeral body up others beneath
No birth changing baby gives birth to mother
Everything happens reply to question long ago set

In the room she sits and sews
Seventeen seventy seven
In the boat he so painfully rows
Nine hundred and ten

This farm man's forcefulness begins in childhood
It rides through adolescence and into manhood
There gathering into a personal and/or social clump
It dazzling leaps forward and achieves nothing or something

No back of the basement
No Egyptian tile replacement
No oaken stuff
Only an under-ample yuan disbursement

The schoolteacher stands
Waving his hand sideways
The car backs in
That brings the Official to his school

No boat no pyramid in this part of town
No float no cinnamon in this part of town
No coast guard in this part of town
No Ecole des Beaux-Arts in this part of town

No fat women
No fat crowds
No fat safety police
No fat fowls

Engine
Sea gull
Fold up
Flash

Amoeba serena
Cows ilk
Uncomprehending
Sample of speech: "Whiff"

What do you write about? "Four Modernizations
Modernization of agriculture, of education
Of industry, of science." The poets' explanation
"We write about the Four Modernizations"

Eternally weather of spring
Sixty-seven degrees temperature sing

No room on airplane Shanghai Kunming
No room on airplane Queylin Hanshu
No soft sleeper
Only hard sleeper journey five days

Suddenly wakes up man room
Bed rumpled dirty several newspaper
Table cup little dishes tea leaves
Meiyou What do you want

Dancers on stage in the theater
Cow at the end of a rope
In the field
Gray dog sitting by a wall

Nothing moving in lifeboat
No one walking in corridor
Only in main salon lobby
Magician describe take handkerchief

Suddenly losing interest
Suddenly losing narrow
Suddenly losing valley
Suddenly losing train

Empty empty
Quiet quiet
Thousand thousand
Sleep and stand

The panda in the Beijing Zoo
Is a minority nationality
The panda in the American zoo
Is overseas Chinese

No snow on the gate to the forbidden city
No snow on the Hall of Felicitous Harmony
No snow on the Pathway of Endless Peace
No sun there either

In and out in and out of traffic goes the car
Drops of rain fall on the Huangpu River
Someone bends forward with anxiety
Another bends back with the machine

When the car comes back
The back seat is empty
When the car sets out
Its seat contains one

Bed is absent
Breast is absent
Bend is absent
Bet is absent

No Western prescriptions
No Vicks VapoRub and no Anacin
No Empirin no Kotex no Trojan rubbers
Only jars of deer horn ground to powder

"Into my brain pattern noxious Occident
Stoop is restful in rain battering uncopying Orient
A glad dry, a roomy husk, pretensions
But later a soothing cry, abrasions, summing up"

Light on water
What is this?
Little boat with light
What light is this?

A man on the boat
A line in the water
A line around the park
Of bushes and trees

The Disappearance of the Turgenev Library

"Farewell, my friends!" said Pushkin, and his eyes turned to his library.
　　　　　　—Vasily Zhukovsky, on Pushkin's death

*N*ovy Mir has published the memoirs of Ilya Ehrenburg, *Years and Men*, a curious work in many respects.[*] There are as many pages devoted to Russian life at the beginning of the century as there are passages on the Cubists and Fauves in Paris, portraits of Modigliani, Picasso, and Diego Rivera, and recollections of Maximilian Voloshin's Parisian period. Before the First World War, Ehrenburg lived in Paris, where he had numerous friends, went everywhere, met celebrities and unknowns, read, wrote poetry. Among other things, he spent many hours in the Turgenev Library. This is what he says:

> I used to borrow books from the Turgenev Library. Its fate was altogether dramatic. In 1875, in Paris, a literary and musical matinée was organized in which Turgenev, Gleb Ouspenski, Pauline Viardot, and the poet Kurochkin participated. In distributing the tickets, Turgenev specified: "The money collected will be used to found a Russian library for the use of needy students." The writer himself donated books, some of

---

[*] *Novy Mir*, 1960, book IX.

which contained annotations in his own hand. Two generations of revolutionaries in exile frequented the *Turgenevka*. Thanks to them, it was enriched with bibliographical rarities. It continued to exist after the revolution; only the readers changed. At the beginning of the Second World War, Russian émigré writers deposited their archives there. One of Hitler's close collaborators, Rosenberg—a Baltic German, considered a great Russophile—moved the library to Germany.

In 1945, shortly before the end of the war, an officer I did not know brought me a letter I had written to M. O. Tsetlin in 1913. He told me he had found some gutted boxes in a German railroad station. Russian letters, books, and manuscripts littered the floor. He had picked up a few letters from Gorky, then, finding my signature at the bottom of a crumbling piece of paper, had decided to do me this favor. Such was the end of the Turgenev Library.

After reading this account, it seemed to me that I too had something to say about the disappearance of the Russian library from Paris. I was there when they removed the books from the old town house that had once belonged to Colbert. The city of Paris had recently put it at the disposal of the *Turgenevka*, which seemed to be ensconced there for eternity. Who could have foreseen its tragic end?

The Germans occupied Paris on June 14, 1940. At the beginning of August, I went there by bicycle: at the time I had a little country house, and a bike was the only available means of transportation. I had left very early, and it was not yet eleven o'clock when I entered the gates of the city.

During that period I used to jot things down, keeping a sort of diary. That day I noted that I had stopped by the Turgenev Library to borrow a volume of Schopenhauer (in Russian translation); then I had seen a documentary film on the Champs-Elysées that showed Hitler and his close associates arriving by car at the place du Trocadéro and contemplating the Eiffel Tower and the Champ-de-Mars. I had spent the night with friends in Boulogne.

A month later, I returned to Paris. This time I went to see Ilya Fondaminsky, who was back from Biarritz and settled in his apartment on the avenue de Versailles.

I don't remember whom he was living with at the time. He still inhabited his dark, damp study, completely lined with books. In August, friends who wanted to hide their belongings had stored many valuable things at my house in the country. Especially paintings. Carefully wrapped in old newspapers and straw, they reposed in the attic: a little Van de Velde, a tall, narrow Boldini. Alexander Benois had also entrusted me with a portfolio of drawings that dated from the seventeenth century. Downstairs, the "living room" housed innumerable transitory friends who were fleeing to the "unoccupied zone"; two or three people sometimes slept there at the same time, and one could glimpse on my shelves, among my modest volumes, the *Russian Portraits* by the Grand Duke Nicolay Mikhailovich, a first edition of Molière's comedies, and other rare books that for a time had found refuge in this corner of France, and that survived. It occurred to me to suggest to Fondaminsky that he leave his valuable books with me to save them from the bombings and house searches that might begin at any moment. But he flatly refused.

Right away, he made fun of me, saying that I was spreading panic. He was not afraid of bombings, for his study was half-buried in the basement. As for searches, they didn't frighten him either, since he had a protector: a young German, a great bibliophile and lover of Russian editions. This man often came to see him in the evening; they talked about everything and nothing. Sometimes, this German (a civilian, if memory serves) also dropped by for a friendly visit during the day. He bought old Russian books at second-hand bookstores and already had an immense collection.

Fondaminsky declared that he felt secure not only about his books but also about his person. There was nothing I could do. I sadly contemplated those shelves full of marvels. I was about to leave when someone knocked on the door. A young man came in, blond, smiling, with a pleasant face and glasses. It was Fondaminsky's new friend.

"Today we have decided to pay a visit to the Turgenev Library," said my host as he introduced us. "I want to show him the beautiful volumes we have there."

I left his place in a state of utter despair.

When I next went to Paris, it was fall. The most difficult aspect of these trips was getting around, burdened as I was with potatoes, milk, and books. So I thought I would first return the volume of Schopenhauer to the *Turgenevka* and leave it with the concierge (the library didn't open until four in the afternoon). That would free me to go to different parts of Paris, see people, do a few errands, and come back when the library had opened.

The Hôtel Colbert is on a little street near Notre-Dame. It was not quite ten o'clock when I entered its portals. The courtyard was filled with rough wooden boxes, long, like coffins—three dozen of them, standing on end or lying flat. They were empty. I knocked on the window of the concierge, who knew me, and asked her if she could keep the book until four o'clock. She gave me a peevish look: "They're here."

I went upstairs at once. The doors were wide open. There were two boxes on the landing, two more in the hall. Quick, efficient, rhythmical gestures: the books were being packed up.

I was stunned. Nevertheless I asked, in my bad German, just what was going on. It was obvious, however. I was answered politely that the books were being sent away. Where? Why? No answer. Suddenly a man appeared in the hall: it was the young collector of Russian editions. He recognized me, and asked, with a smile, if he could be of any help.

My emotions must have been written all over my face. He took a step toward me. I thought he wanted to take the Schopenhauer from me. No doubt I would have given it to him. But he was not at all interested in the book I held under my arm. On the contrary. He asked, amiably and with a sort of compassion, if there were any books of mine in the library. He would return them to me at once. I didn't quite grasp what he meant: did he intend, knowing that I was a writer, to give me back the books I had written? Or the books that belonged to me? I left him standing there and I departed.

Once back downstairs, I remembered that, indeed, being short of funds, I had left there as security my *Armenian Poetry*, a thick volume published under Valery Bryusov's editorship; they must have kept it in one of the back rooms, in case I should lose a book. This had been a good twelve years earlier. But I did not go back to get it.

The young collector had worked out his plan of action long before calling on Fondaminsky. He knew perfectly well that there was a Russian library in Paris. I was sure of this, but I didn't relish the prospect of going to Fondaminsky's. I had the feeling that we could still try to do something. How? After a moment's hesitation, I hurried to Vasily Alexandrovich Maklakov's place, in Montparnasse.

I had been to see him often since the start of the war. Despondent, he welcomed visitors with open arms. His hearing was getting worse and worse, and his hearing aid (one of the early models) refused to work, so you had to shout into his ear. Every time the telephone or doorbell rang, light bulbs lit up on the ceiling of his study. This got on my nerves. But there was also something cozy and comfortable about his apartment: was it his sister trotting about so quietly, or the elderly maid, or the objects, the books, and the papers that filled his study? He greeted me, dressed in a velvet jacket, astonished and happy to see me at that hour.

After I'd told him what had just taken place, he thought for a few moments. Then he looked at me. It was at that moment that the same idea simultaneously crossed our minds, as often happens. We had thought of the same thing.

"I know where we have to go," he said. "You know, too."

I nodded without saying anything.

"We must alert the Soviet Embassy; after all, they are Germany's ally. They'd be able to intervene. Providing, of course, we find the right person and explain it to him properly. They'll put a stop to all that."

A moment later, he was calling the president of the Turgenev Library's administrative staff, D. M. Odinets, the historian and collaborator on Paul Milyukov's periodical, *The Latest News.* Odinets joined us a half-hour later.

I was obliged to repeat my story. Maklakov had removed his hearing aid, which exhausted him, and sat at his desk taking no further part in our conversation. Odinets agreed with us: the only thing to do was to go to the rue de Grenelle and ask the Soviets to intervene.

"Who should go?" I asked.

"It's my responsibility," Odinets replied.

We had a quick snack, and he left. I stayed and waited for him.

I might say, looking ahead, that Odinets came to a sad end. We had known each other for a long time. When he had an operation (during the war), I often went to visit him at the Val-de-Grâce hospital where he was recuperating in a municipal ward. He was suffering from malnutrition; at that time, there were serious food shortages. His charming young daughter prepared hot chocolate for him on a hot plate placed on his bedside table. He drank it right out of the pot, while the other patients watched him with envy. She made some for them, too. Scarcely had he recovered from his operation, in 1944, when he put his name on the list of Soviet patriots and soon left for the U.S.S.R. Authorized to live in Kazan, he died there a few years later.

But that day, at Maklakov's, nothing allowed one to foresee such an unlikely end for an émigré, an anti-Bolshevik Russian. Maklakov, on edge, paced from room to room. I sat in his study and tried to distract myself by reading an old roster of the members of the Duma: their brief biographies, with their dates of birth, the party they belonged to . . . Vasily Alexandrovich came toward me, looking angry:

"A long time ago, I scratched out my date of birth with a knife. Now it doesn't matter to me at all. So people know I'm an old man! What difference can it make? Here, I'll write it in. Or write it in yourself."

"I'll do nothing of the sort! Let it stay the way it is. Anyway, where do you expect me to write? There's nothing but a hole."

During that first year of war, and even the following one, he didn't really look old. It was after being in a German prison that he went completely downhill. He told me later that when he was being released from prison all he could think about was his shoelaces, which they hadn't returned to him. He pictured himself in the street, his shoes undone and his pants falling off, since they had also kept his belt. And as he'd gotten very thin in the Santé (despite the packages sent by his friends), he was afraid of losing his pants. All this concerned him far more than his freedom.

Odinets returned after two hours. I jotted down his report as he spoke. At the embassy they had shown him into one room, then into another. He had asked to see the first secretary, or the first consul, or, if possible, the ambassador himself. He had spoken with one person, then another, then a third, without their having introduced themselves. He had had to explain several times the purpose of his visit: to save the Russian library. Turgenev had founded it . . . the author of *Fathers and Sons* and *Rudin*, when he was living in Paris . . . But their faces were blank. It was vital to act fast, before the books were taken away . . . But these people simply shrugged their shoulders: "How does this concern us? Emigré dramatics!"

"All of a sudden," Odinets said, "I had an inspiration. I hit upon . . . 'Lenin,' I said, 'worked in this library. There are books here with annotations in his own hand in the margins, and others that he left to the library. Even his chair is here!' "

Never before, he admitted, had his imagination worked so hard.

"Everyone started running around me and getting excited. They called in three more people. I had to repeat what I'd just told them about Lenin."

He ended his account by saying:

"They showed me out through another set of doors. They kept opening and shutting them. Someone promised me he would intervene, but I don't really believe it. And to think that one telephone call might have done the trick!"

That night I stayed again with my friends in Boulogne. The next day, when I got to the Hôtel Colbert, it was all over. The coffins were gone, the doors closed and sealed. The largest Russian library in exile had ceased to exist.

I never saw Fondaminsky again. I kept the Schopenhauer.[*]

Translated by Patsy Southgate

[*] Thanks to the work of devoted volunteers, part of the funding for rebuilding a Russian library in Paris has been raised, little by little, over the postwar years. We continue to gather books. The new collection has as its foundation the duplicate copies (nearly six hundred volumes) that were stored in the Hôtel Colbert's basement, to which the Germans did not have access. The city of Paris has put a new building at the library's disposal.

Visceral Reluctance

The late world stands fixed. It's an easy
distant chalice to be sure of where you
art. I'll be throwing you, the amateur
table salt clenched in DOS, specialty talk
rounding off the veneer. Where you are.

By the way. I'm efficient as any writer
dealing with an ailing laughter, the rhyme
with "on the lam" mustered and split.
Falling asleep in my chair, I preserve
a measure of flexibility: swivel power.

This penchant for dorsal humidity collects
and impossibly sizes, a rapt hint in a broken
contaminant span. We push stalemate to its
logical profusion: there's very little a word
won't portray in a slow note to the behooved.

Bend it off and broach, then slash to the nearest
element, a windshield kind of recession argues
integration with a background of candy benday.
More of those grumbles will have to be put back there
so that the business can be carried out as such.

It's a stall, the kind of veering crush that spins
the listener full cycle, emptying dime novels of all
but their deeds. Mistakes in this environment look
like candles. A throw rug hangs from the spool.
Forms chisel, and the microscopic languor in serum

Binds the alternatives. Wholly open to them, that's how
the major players claim to be, but behind each window
a teller sorts the slips, affixed to the lonely rack
of a crabby fussbudget. Golden apples of our summer's work
lie scattered on a table of wood and stone, a reckoning.

A reason not to stands against the hail in blended mass.
A recondite solution drains the bill of nonchalance
and switches, done for a ducat, halfway home from the corporation
yard, because there isn't any, only a serial semblance of make,
model, method, mask, and means, the total slipping by instances.

The early warning runs up a task. It's a hard
tight interior where you can only turn around
a lot. I'll be heaving into view, the professional
chairperson properly decked in muck, generalities
ripping off the air. Which is not how *you* are.

On Cithaeron

A wild slope of Mount Cithaeron. OEDIPUS *enters, led by*
ANTIGONE. *They are tired and pause to rest.*

OEDIPUS [*To* ANTIGONE]
Guide, nurse, crutch . . . What a daughter you are,
worth the enormous trouble of your begetting!
Leave me, I pray, or rather command, for prayer
doesn't sit well in my mouth. I am accursed
as no man ever was before. Go, go,
let me stumble and grope my way to find
that elusive step for which my soul and soles
are tingling with desire. I see the darkness
and wish to hear and feel it also—the great
nothing. The light I am blind to finds me out.
Let go my hand; leave it to better employment.
My own Cithaeron calls me, its rugged crags
eager to finish that job of work they began
a lifetime ago. My life should have ended then
in these wild defiles. To these same slopes Actaeon
came with his hounds, beheld the naked goddess,
was turned into a stag, and felt their rough
embrace as they mauled and tore his flesh to prove
him merely mortal. To these foothills Agave
led the way for her sister-priestesses

105

and together in their enthusiastic revels
they tore apart her darling son and, shrieking,
held the head aloft on a sacred wand.
On these same slopes, the untamed bull ran raging,
dragging what at first was Dirce, and then
was what she had been, and by and by became
anonymous mere meat—and Zetus smiled
as he followed the bloody track and watched the swift
declension of his revenge. To those high cliffs
that tower over the sea and make the knees
melt with their giddy height, poor Ino came,
fleeing before Athamas' fury, and leapt,
her babe in her arms, into the insubstantial
air and the waiting rocks and water below.
Compared to mine, their fates were gentle, sweet,
and enviable, for I survived that death
my father contrived for me, to endure much worse—
a lifetime's pain, and bitter shame, and griefs
unmatched in all the world. To these sweet woods
I now return to claim that favor of mercy
the fates snatched from the grasp of my infant fists.
My proper place is here. Now am I home
among true kin—cruelty, savagery, blood,
fierce when they kill, and more fierce when they spare,
as some cats will for a time, the lives of their prey.

    Let my hand go! My father summons
his son, and I come. His blood calls out to mine.
My love for you is all that holds me back.
I detest my life. It sticks in my soul's craw,
and I want only to vomit out its poison.

ANTIGONE
No power in the world could tear me from you,
neither human nor divine. I cling
to what I love. Let my poor brothers quarrel
over the spoils of our noble house. Its richest
treasure I keep to myself—my own dear father.
Eteocles on the throne and Polynices
encamped at the gates wrangle over trifles.

Wealth and power are toys of children when love
is weighed against them. Jupiter's thunderbolts
could not loosen my grip on your hand. Not even
you may forbid me. Go where you will, I'll guide
your unwilling feet—to mountain crest or plain,
along familiar paths or through wild brambles,
at the edges of dizzying cliffs where death gapes
far below. I'll walk with you even there,
and still, with hand in hand, we'll plunge together,
or I'll go first, my eyes to direct your feet,
your will to direct my eyes. Whatever you choose,
that shall content and delight me. I shall demand
nothing, oppose nothing—not even death,
if that is what you desire. Live or perish,
I follow and obey, as the parts of your body
perform what your mind decrees, your muscle and bone.
Only feel their strength which is your own.
Take heart from the burdens you've borne and even the shame.
There comes at last defiance, a kind of pride
in not having been crushed. Hold your head high,
the king not merely of Thebes but of grief itself.
To give in to your woes would be to die.

OEDIPUS

In a sinful house, whence comes this sport of virtue?
That I should produce a loving child is madness.
Surely, the gods mock me. Nature is playing
jokes. Rivers as soon will flow uphill,
and Apollo's torch usher in the gloom of night.
The cream of the jest will be my elevation
to sanctity, my foulness somehow transformed
to holiness by the love of this wide-eyed girl.
Do I weep or laugh? My eyes have no tears left,
and want only one thing now—that my poor father's
death may be avenged at last by my own.
You mean well, girl, but you only increase my pain,
for I am a corpse that yearns for the cover of earth.
My shadow stains the road; I offend the sun.
To kill someone who wishes to live is evil;

it is just as bad to keep a person alive
whose desire it is to die. I count it worse,
the pain of despair being worse than any death.
For your love's sake, and pity's, let me go.
No longer sovereign of Thebes, I am yet master
of my own life and death. Companion and friend,
give me my sword, that famous weapon I held
when I killed my father. Put it into my hand,
to use on myself, to use on my sons, to cut
in a blind frenzy at foulness that's everywhere!
My soul is on fire—build me a funeral pyre
on which I can fling myself, to embrace the cleansing
flames that will set me free. I can taste the ashes.
Or lead me to that cliff you spoke of. The blue
water below will wash away my sins,
tumbling in brine the corruptible flesh
until there is only the white brightness of bone.
On such a cliff, the Sphinx once sat and glowered,
and there I showed how smart I was with an answer
to her child's riddle. With the Fates' much harder riddle,
I performed less well, until, with many hints,
I groaned out my heartbroken reply. Lead me
to that stone seat where I shall sit and amaze
the passersby, until one comes enraged
or disgusted enough to fling my feeble ruin
over the edge. But mothers will put to their children
my deplorable riddle, the worst the world has ever
propounded—and they all will know the answer.
He was his own grandfather's son-in-law;
his father's rival; his sons' and daughters' brother;
his brothers' father. At one astonishing moment,
the grandmother brought forth to her husband children,
and to herself grandchildren. Who was he?
They'll giggle of course, as children will, at the joke,
which is what they make of the monstrous. Master of riddles,
I couldn't master this one. In all Thebes,
I was the last to guess the dismal answer.
O my daughter, what can you say to console,
to hearten this battered hulk you lead about

like a dancing bear? Your gentle words would be welcome
to any heart, but mine is utterly dead,
a dull and heavy stone in a stupid chest
that continues to breathe. No night is dark enough
for me to hide in. Deep Tartarus itself
will recoil, I have no doubt, when I arrive
in something like the greeting I've grown used to
here in this life. You could not protect me from that
and cannot keep from me the release I seek,
for Death is everywhere. The gods in their wisdom
have arranged the affairs of men so that one may rob
a person of his life but not of his death.
Swords and nooses abound, and cliffs and ravines,
and venomous adders lurking in deadly plants.
To the hall of the dead, they say a thousand doors
gape in grisly welcome. I will enter,
by one or another, or let it enter me,
for no part of my body is free from taint.
All is corruption, my fingers and hands, my blood,
my manhood and my heart. They all cry out
for mortal blows. My eyes that have wept red gore
blink in the expectation of new assaults.
I stand before my father that he may choose
what is the proper penalty and atonement.
Wherever you are, signal to me your will.
I am a novice yet of griefs and pains.
Decree whatever further sacrifices
my crimes require and I shall perform them all,
turning my bloodied hand upon myself.
Your hatred for me cannot exceed my own
self-loathing. Come to my aid and guide
my all but nerveless hand, and I shall strike
again, and deeper, having botched before
what ought to have been a final obliteration
not merely of sight but of life itself.
After the boldness with which I had sinned, my timid
attempt upon myself was contemptible, mean,
and childish. I am filled with shame to think
by how far short I fell. Beyond the orbs

of the eyes there was the brain which should have been
obliterated. There was the world I wanted
to uncreate. Oblivion I wanted,
or the world's primal chaos, that primal murk
in which my lust and savagery could hide.
The sockets were the door. I brought myself
up to the threshold but fell back, a coward.
Now, in disgust and rage, I am ready to cross.

ANTIGONE

O great of soul, I beg you, father, consider!
Listen to me, your wretched loving daughter.
Those thunderstorms of the passions are all behind you,
as distant as the grandeur of your throne.
We look down as a pair of soaring birds
on tiny creatures we know to be men and women,
animated by joys and sorrows we scarcely
credit now, indifferent as we are
and safe—for there is safety *in extremis*.
Beyond all hope and fear, not even the gods
can affect you further. You have borne their utmost
and lived. You have survived, despising death's
easy evasions. That burden would have crushed
an ordinary man. You threw away
the blessing men desire and have endured
more than what men fear in their worst nightmares.
Your prize is a great detachment: you may look down
purged, perfected, purified, your heart
hardened to shining diamond and disconnected
from all those ties that trammel men: your throne,
your palace, native city, mother, sons,
and even the light of day are all forgone
if not forgotten. What death can take away
you have let go already. What can its darkness
hold out for you in threat or promise of freedom
that your life has not already given? Having lost
all, you have lost all taint and blemish. The murmur
of castle and court has given way to the silence
of temple and tomb, with the long songs of the wind

as reverent descant. What can you imagine
from death that can tempt you further? That great quiet
is in your heart already. Only listen,
attend to the wisdom you have so dearly bought,
the grand indifference that I have learned from you.

OEDIPUS

I flee myself. And consciousness. I flee
my hands, my crimes, the sky, the gods, the earth
my feet offend, the air my breathing fouls,
the sweet water the touch of my cursed lips
pollutes. I flee the limitless disgust
I feel for my existence. The world's good order
I have defied, defiled. The one gift left
within my power would be to undo the offense
and erase myself from the slate of the universe.
The tenderest words of men and women affront
my ears when I hear them: parent, brother, child
set me apart as the monstrous one. I long
for utter silence, blank as the perfect darkness
I've drawn about me like a shroud. But guilt
can ravel that. It's consciousness I hate
and want to be rid of at last.
                                             And you, my daughter,
I want to be rid of you, for you remind me
what I have done and am, being who you are
and what you are to me. You mean no harm,
but the harm is done, is there. Your gentle voice
indicts, your caring touch burns like a brand,
and I turn away in loathing from what I love.
I cannot hide from my own unspeakable evil,
have peeled away the outer leaves of my life—
kingdom, parents, children, my famous wit,
even my senses—but what remains offends
nevertheless: the onion's tears. Of these,
I have also stripped myself to the mere idea,
which is hateful still. For pity's sake, away!
There is nothing for you to say. I will not listen.
I am like a stretched cord that vibrates response

to the sound of one note only—that of my fate
which all along has waited for me. An infant,
I was doomed already. My first cry was that one
baleful note. Or before then, in the womb,
I terrified my parents, who knew from the omens
that what I brought was disaster, disgrace, a ruin
like none that had gone before. Other children have died
at birth, or even before, but the taint of sin
has not attached to these. I was born guilty,
set out on the mountainside, and left to the mercy
of savage beasts and Cithaeron's birds of prey
thirsty for my blood. And death itself
disdained me, turned away as if in horror
of what I was fated to do, or as if to dare
such terrible things to come to pass in the world.
Would the brat survive, would he commit
those crimes that had been foretold for him? He would!
I did. Like a puppet, I acted out the awful
guignol plot I could not escape, the strings
working my hands and feet and mind and heart
as if it were a natural thing for a son
to creep into his father's bed with his hands
still red with that father's blood and there,
as reward for the one offense, commit a worse.

    It was nothing to kill my father—or nothing much
compared to what followed, unnatural, affronting
nature itself. My very penance turned
to further and worse crime—I flung away
my father's scepter as if it were burning hot,
and what was the result? My sons are fighting,
a pair of curs greedy for one bone
and ready to kill. Eteocles refuses
to honor their agreement, and Polynices
brings his Argive host to Thebes to shed
the blood of his native city. The widows, the orphans,
the maimed soldiers, the raped maidens and matrons
will hate those two, but put the blame on me,
the begetter of all their troubles. Thebes is sick
of me and my house, the city I love hates me,

as it ought to do, and as I do myself.
All that I ever loved or touched, I've ruined.

ANTIGONE

But father, think! If you need a reason to live,
consider what you have just said. Who can better
talk to those two to restrain them? A father's command
may yet avert the threat of war. Your word
must resonate with authority. They'll listen—
to father, brother, king, and holy man.
That death you crave for yourself will be widespread.

OEDIPUS

Why would they listen to me? They are both of them mad,
power-mad, the blood-lust up, accursed.
They are my sons, brought into this world
by evil and for evil. They outdo one another
in wickedness. They surpass even myself,
for they are beyond shame. Their passions drive them
headlong toward whatever goal their greed
and lust present. They are monstrous sons of a monster.
Their destiny is another reason for me
to want to die, in order that I may avoid
the further guilts they will bring upon my house
and upon my head. Destruction seems a kind
alternative. Daughter, daughter, don't.
Don't fall to your knees, do not grasp mine, do not
weep with gentle tears to seek my further
pain. I am resolved. My quarrel with fate
is easily resolved. I can walk away,
simply refuse to participate any further,
and decline to be. The only ray in the bleak
ruin of my existence has been yourself.
From moment to moment, the single thing preventing
my suicide has been the comfort that you
have always offered, that understanding love
I would not otherwise believe existed.
For you alone I have drawn my painful breaths.

[A MESSENGER *enters and bows.*]

MESSENGER
I greet you great lord, and bring you news of Thebes
which calls you to her aid. Brother and brother
brandish their weapons and threaten deadly battle.
Only you can prevent the slaughter. We beg you,
return home to separate your sons
and impose as a father can, and as a king,
a peace between them. For piety's sake we plead,
do us this last great service, Oedipus.

OEDIPUS
What are you asking? Whom are you asking? Prevent
crimes, sins, outrages? Has something happened
to alter my appearance? I am no teacher
of piety and justice. I am a sinner,
blood and guilt are my métier. I applaud
their dreadful continuation of my sad story.
They are my sons, my boys, chips off the old
sacrificial altar, red with gore.
I urge them on. Let them commit offenses
to dwarf my own. Let them inscribe their names
in the annals of evil in such huge letters that mine
will hardly occasion remark. Our noble house
is famous for this. Let them prove their mettle,
their high birth. The gods have their eyes upon us,
and what we do astonishes mankind.
I take a perverse pride. Let them spill their
blood and everyone else's. Let them bring down
our house in spectacular ruin, and let them know,
as I have, the cold comfort of extreme
despair.

ANTIGONE
Father, restrain yourself. You play
with grief. My brothers need you. Thebes does. Go
and tell them to give over their vain ambitions.

OEDIPUS

I am no gentle sage! What is this nonsense?
I am enraged! A bitter, desperate man,
full of the blackness of grief and that of hate,
I cannot tell where one gives way to the other.
It's all black—the universe is the darkness
I stare at every moment! Let Polynices
rush upon Eteocles, and let them erase
a part of what I imposed upon the revolted
earth. Let outrage compound outrage. A brother
kills a brother? Better, give your mother
a sword and let her shed the too rich blood
of children and grandchildren. I'll hide in a cave
and wait to hear what happens and howl. And howl.

Translated by David R. Slavitt

Mercy Seat

—for Billie Holiday

The Café Society was a cottonless plantation
where she sang *hunger* and *love* like nobody
else. Like nobody else she was beautifully used
as motor oil through the overheated engine
on the bus from Baltimore to the custody
of men. For all our frictions, the blues—
the great mother-hugging blues.

    She'd come out of the dark like a forced bloom
    fed on smack, Satchmo, and the frayed edges of Jim Crow.

The black body scarred and the black body lost
in the smoke, the ark, the few tables, the perfumes.
The body chopped and cooked into a voice,
the voice shot up into a face,
that spectacle, that shroud, that half-
owned, half-turned thing, the greasy pig of the self.

    She'd come out in her satin and sing,
    bow, then leave us to ourselves.

This was the plumb and pendulum of swing,
the strange fruit swinging from the poplar trees,
for the sun to rot . . .
and the wind to suck . . . in A-flat,
ba-deep, ba-dop, Go as far as you can go, girl.
After every show in the USO tour, for the smell
of a woman they would pick her gardenia to pieces,
petal by petal.

Homely Girl,
A Life

Janice awoke feeling cold that Monday morning, which was odd—a wind seemed to blow on her as she surfaced from a deep sleep, already recalling it was June and yesterday had been warm in Central Park. And opening her eyes as usual toward him she saw how strangely blanched his face was, although what she called his sleeping smile was still there, and the usual suggestion of happiness at the curled corners of his mouth. But he seemed heavier on the mattress. She knew immediately, and with dread she raised her hand and touched his cheek—the end of the long story. Her first thought, like an appeal against a mistake: "But he is only sixty-eight!"

Fright but no tears, not outside. Just the thump on the back of her neck. Life had a fist.

"Ah!" she pitied aloud and, bringing her palms together, touched her fingers to her lips. "Ah!" She bent to him, her silky hair touching his face. But he wasn't there. "Ah, Charles!" A little anger, soon dispersed by reason. And wonder.

The wonder remained. That after all her life had amounted to a little something, had given her this man, this man who had never seen her. He was awesome now, lying there.

Oh, if one more time she could have spoken with him, asked or told him . . . what? The thing in her heart, the wonder. That he had loved her and had never seen her in the fourteen years of their life. There was always, despite everything, something within her trying to move itself into his line of vision, as though with one split-second glimpse of her his fluttering eyes would wake from their eternal sleep.

Now what do I do? Oh, Charles dear, what do I do with the rest of it?

Something was not finished. But I suppose, she said to herself, nothing ever is except in movies when the lights come on, leaving you squinting on the sidewalk.

Once more she moved to touch him, but already he was not there, not hers, not anything, and she withdrew her hand and sat there with one leg hanging over the mattress.

•   •   •

She hated her face as a girl but knew she had style and at least once a day settled for that and her very good compact body and a terrific long neck. And yes, her irony. She was and wanted to be a snob. She knew how to slip a slight, witty rotation into her hips when she walked, although she had no illusions it made up for a pulled look to her cheeks, as if alum had tightened her skin, and an elongated upper lip. A little like Disraeli, she thought once, coming on his picture in a high school text. And a too-high forehead (she refused to overlook anything negative). She wondered if she'd been drawn out of the womb and lengthened, or her mother startled by a giraffe. At parties she had many a time noticed how men coming up behind her were caught surprised when she turned to face them. But she had learned to shake out the straight silky light brown hair and flick the ironic defensive grin, silent pardon for their inevitable fade. She had a tonic charm and it was almost enough—although not quite, of course, not since childhood, when her mother held up a *Cosmopolitan* Ivory ad to her face and so warmly and lovingly exclaimed, "Now that's beauty!" as though by staring at it hard enough she could be made to look like one of those girls. She felt blamed then. Still, at fifteen she believed that between her ankles and her breasts she was as luscious as Betty Grable, or almost. And she had a soft provocative lisp that men who had an interest in mouths seemed to like. When she was sixteen Aunt Ida, visiting from Egypt, had said, "You've got an Egyptian look, Egyptian women are hot." Recalling that oddity would make her laugh and would raise her spirits even into her sixties after Charles had died.

A number of memories involved lying in bed on a Sunday morning, listening thankfully to muffled New York outside. "I was just thinking—apropos of nothing," she said once, speaking softly into Charles's ear, "that for at least a year after Sam and I had separated I was terribly embarrassed to say we had. And even after you and I married, whenever I had to refer to 'my first husband' it curdled something inside me. It was like a disgrace or a defeat. What a simple-minded generation we were!"

Sam was beneath her in some indefinite class sense, but that was part of his attraction in the thirties, when to have been born into money was shameful, a guarantee of futility. People her age, early twenties then, wanted to signify by doing good, attending emergency meetings a couple of times a week in downtown lofts or sympathizers' West End Avenue living rooms to raise money for organizing the new National Maritime Union or ambulances for the Spanish Republicans, and they were moved to genuine outrage by Fascism, which was somehow a parents' system and the rape of the mind; the Socialist hope was for the young, for her, and no parent could help fearing its subversive beauty. Anyway, hers were hopelessly silly people, Jews putting on the dog with a new absurd name endowed by the immigration inspectors back in the other century because great-grandpa's original Russian one was unpronounceable by their Irish tongues. So they were Sessions.

But Sam was Fink, which she rather relished as a taunt to her father, long a widower and very ill now but still being consulted on the phone as an authority on utilities by the time of her marriage, dying as he read that Hitler had walked into Vienna. "But he won't last," he whispered scoffingly across the cancer in his throat, "the Germans are too intelligent for this idiot." But of course by now she knew better, knew a world was ending and would not be surprised to see American storm troopers with chin straps on Broadway one evening. It was already scary to go walking around in Yorkville on the Upper East Side where the Germans were rallying on the streetcorners to bait Jews and praise Hitler on summertime Saturday nights. She was not particularly Semitic-looking, but she feared the fear of the prey as she passed thick-necked men on 86th Street.

A stylish man, her father, with a long noble head and an outmoded mind, or so she thought of him in the flush of her new-found revolutionary independence. Stroking his cold hand in the gloom of the West End Avenue apartment she thanked her luck, or rather her own perceptive intelligence, for having helped turn her away from all this heavy European silverware, the overstuffed chairs and the immense expanse of Oriental carpet, the sheer doomed weight of their possessions and the laughable confidence it had once expressed. If not beautiful, she was at least strong, free of Papa's powerful illusions. But now that he was weak and his eyes were closed most of the time, she could let herself admit that she shared his arrogant style, caring a lot and pretending not to, unlike her mother, who'd screamingly pretended to care and hadn't at all. But of course Papa accepted the injustice in the world as natural, like trees, while for her it was often an unbearable waste. An outwardly conventional man, he was quickly bored by predictable people and had linked her to him by his secret mockery of uniformity, which had fueled her rebellion against her mother. A day before he died he smiled at her and said, "Don't worry, Janice, you're pretty enough, you'll be ok, you've got the guts." If only ok could ever be enough.

The rabbi's brief ceremony must have been developed for these bankrupt times; people were scanting even those rote funerary farewells to get back to their gnawing make-a-living worries. Following the prayer the funeral chapel man, looking like H. L. Mencken with hair parted in the middle, shot his starched cuffs and picked up the small cardboard box of ashes, handing it to her fat brother, Herman, who in his surprise looked at it like it was a ticking explosive. Then they went out into the hot sunlit street and walked downtown together. Herman's butterball wife, Edna, kept falling behind to look into an occasional shoestore window, one of the few still occupied in whole blocks of vacancies along Broadway. Half of New York seemed to be for rent, with permanent signs announcing vacancies bolted to nearly every apartment house. Herman walked flopping his feet like a seal and sucked for breath. "Look at it, the whole block," he said with a wave of his hand.

"Real estate doesn't interest me right now," Janice said.

"Oh, it doesn't? Maybe eating does, cause this is where Papa put a lot of your money, Baby."

They sat at a darkened Irish bar on 84th Street facing Broadway with an electric fan blowing into their faces. "Did you hear? Roosevelt's supposed to have syph."

"I'm trying to drink this, please." Defying ritual and capitalist superstition, she wore a beige skirt and a shiny white silk blouse and high-heeled tan shoes. Sam had to be in Syracuse to bid on an important library being auctioned. "You must be the last Republican Jew in New York," she said.

Herman wheezed, absently moving the little box around on the bar like the final beleaguered piece in a lost chess game, a futile three inches in one direction and then in the other. He sipped his beer and talked about Hitler, the remorseless heat that summer, and real estate.

"These refugees are coming over and buying up Amsterdam Avenue."

"So what difference does that make?"

"Well, they're supposed to be so downtrodden."

"You want them more downtrodden? Don't you understand anything? Now that Franco's won, Hitler's going to attack Russia, there's going to be a tremendous war. And all you can think of is real estate."

"So what if he attacks Russia?"

"Oh God, I'm going home." Disgust flowed up her back and, glancing at the little box, she drank her second martini fast. How really weird, she thought, a whole man fitting into a four-by-six-inch carton hardly big enough for a few muffins.

"If you'd throw some of your share in with mine, we could pick up buildings for next to nothing. This depression won't last forever and we could clean up someday."

"You really know how to pick a time to talk about business." He had all Papa's greed but with a baby face and none of his charm. Slipping off her stool, smiling angrily, she gave him a monitory bop on the head with her purse, kissed Edna's plump

cheek, and with heels clacking walked into the street, Herman behind her defending his right to be interested in real estate.

She was halfway home in the taxi when she recalled that at some point he had bequeathed the ashes to her. Had he remembered to take them from the bar? She called him. Scandalized, he piped, "You mean you lost them?" She hung up, cutting him off, scared. She had left Papa on the bar. She went weak in the knees, surprised by some superstitious fear that she had to force out of her mind. After all, she thought, what is the body? Only the *idea* of a person matters, and Papa's in my heart. Running a bath and flowing toward transcendence again in the remnants of her yellow martini haze, she glimpsed her unchangeable face in the steamy mirror, and the body mattered. Yet at the same time it didn't. She tried to recall a classical philosopher who might have reconciled the two truths, but she tired of the effort. Then, realizing she had bathed only a few hours earlier, she shut off the tap and began to dress.

She found she was hurrying and knew she had to get the ashes back; she had done an awful thing leaving them there, something like sin. For a moment her father lived, reprimanding her with his saddened look. But why, despite everything, was there something funny in the whole business? How tasteless she was.

The bartender, a thin, long-armed man, recalled no such box. He asked if there was anything valuable in it and she said, "Well, no." Then the guilt butted her like a goat. "My father. His ashes."

"Holy Jesus!" The man's eyes widened at this omen of bad luck. His flaring emotion startled her into weeping. It was the first time and she felt grateful to him, and also ashamed that he might feel more about Papa than she did. He touched her back with his hand and guided her to the dismal ladies room in the rear, but looking around she found nothing. He was odorless, like Vaseline, and for a split second she wondered if this were all a dream. She stared down at the toilet. Oh God, what if someone sprinkled Papa down there! Returning to the bar, she touched the man's thick tattooed forearm. "It doesn't matter," she reassured him. He insisted on giving her a drink and she had a martini, and they talked about different kinds of death, sudden and drawn-out, the deaths of the very young and the old. Her eyes were red-rimmed. Two gas-company workers at the bar listened in brutal solemnity from a respectful distance. It had always been more relaxing for her to be among strange men than among women she didn't know. The bartender came around the bar to see her to the door, and before she could think she kissed him on the cheek. "Thank you," she said. Sam had never really pursued her, she thought now, she had more or less granted herself to him. She walked down Broadway, angry and regretful about their marriage, but by the time she reached the corner loved, or at least pitied, him again.

And so Papa was gone. After a few blocks she felt relieved as she sensed the gift of mourning in her, that illusion of connection with a past; but how strange that the emotion should have been given her by a Catholic Irishman who probably supported Franco and couldn't stand Jews. Everything was feeling, nothing was clear. Somehow, in this unexpected confrontation with the barman's direct feeling, she saw that she really must stop waiting to become someone else: she was Janice forever. What an exciting idea! If she could follow it maybe it would lead her to solid ground. It was like the Depression itself—everybody kept waiting for it to lift and forgot how to live in the meantime. But supposing it went on forever? She must start living! And Sam had to stop thinking so exclusively about Fascism and organizing unions and the rest of the endlessly repetitive radical agenda. . . . But she mustn't think that way, she guiltily corrected herself.

She smiled, thinking of her new liberation. In a few minutes, walking down Broadway, she saw something amusing in so formal and fastidious a man as Dave Sessions being left in a box on a bar—she could see him trapped in there, tiny, outraged and red-faced, banging on the lid to be let out. A strange thought struck her—that the body was more of an abstraction than the soul, which never disappeared.

204 Messages to K.

K. went
to the continent
suddenly
leaving
an answering machine
to record
my first attempt

Hello, K.
Just called to say hello

My second attempt

K. Hello
Just wanted
to go over
a coupla things

My third attempt

K. I have missed
your mellifluous voice

My fourth attempt

K. K. K. K.
Your knowledge
of science and automobiles

is beating
my eardrums
like bees

K.
your teaching
natural chemistry
in the tin schoolhouse
to the cream
of the country kids
in Arima, Trinidad

invades my dreams

I now have car
and mate
and I'm swooning
over possible
boys and girls
shooting out
of our house

K., I have one hundred
and ninety nine things
left to tell you.

Anatomy

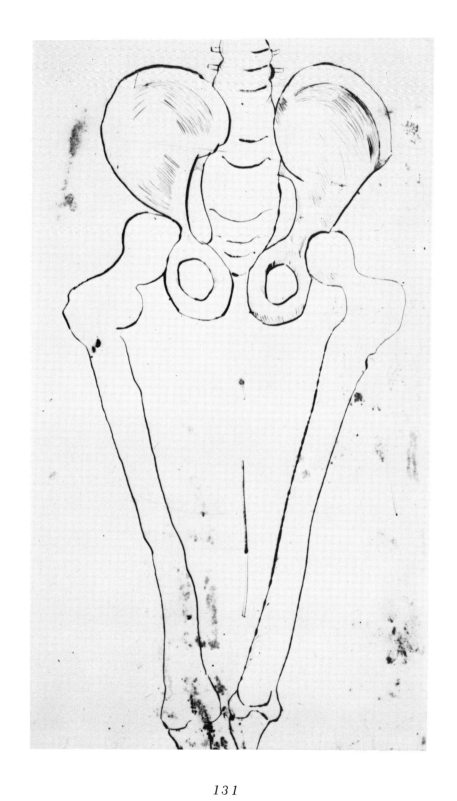

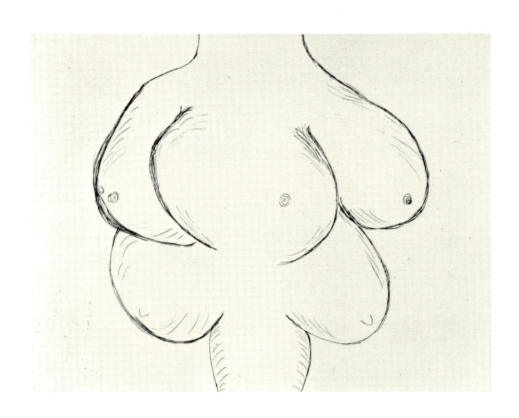

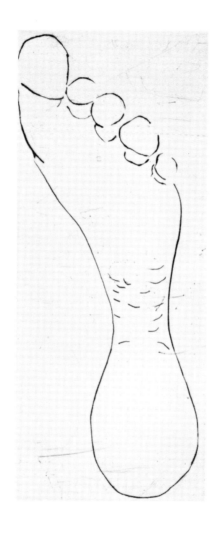

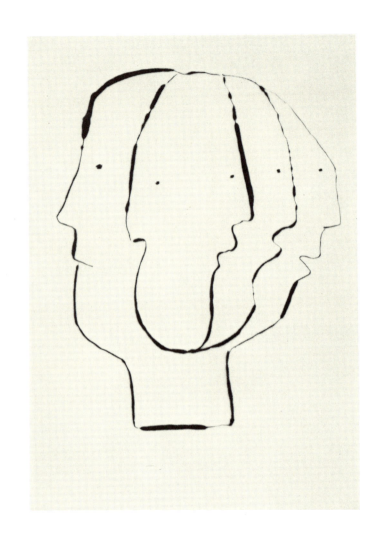

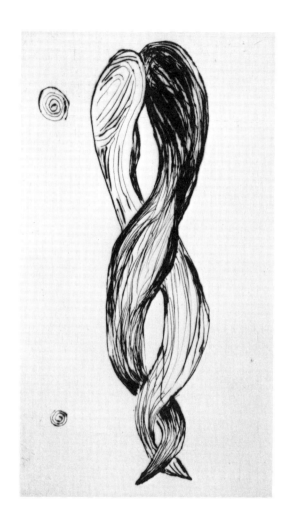

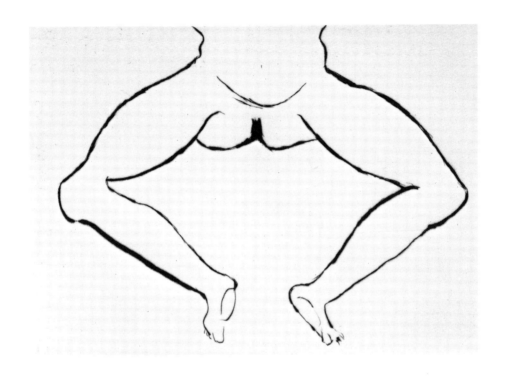

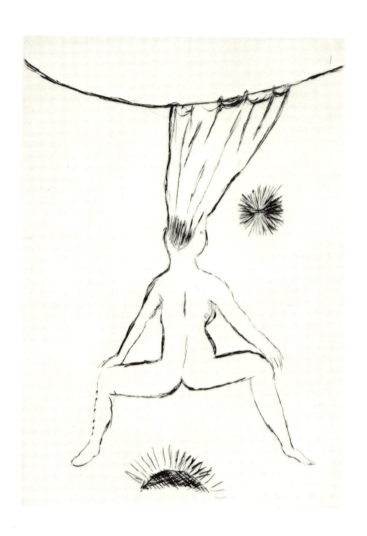

39/44

L B.

Anatomy

The preceding images make up the boxed portfolio *Anatomy*, 1989–90, by Louise Bourgeois. The portfolio contains eleven prints in etching and drypoint on Somerset soft white paper. One (p. 131) measures 25 x 18 in.; the others (pp. 132–41) are 19½ x 14 in. Plate images rather than full sheets are reproduced. In addition, each portfolio contains one multiple on paper (p. 143), which measures 11 x 8½ in.

The edition consists of forty-four copies with each print and multiple signed and numbered in Arabic numbers, and an additional ten copies signed and numbered in Roman numerals. Published by Peter Blum Edition, New York.

Hotel Atlantic

I

The lungs, being the seat of sadness,
Which Victorian memories spew forth,
Occasioned by a weakness taken in that seat.

A malformed woman in a pen and lighter shop,
Fat German waiters
In a railway hotel—when I had come to smoke Tobacco.

A deformed woman who never
Sold me a lighter,
Never sold me a pen.
I exchanged greetings with her when
I passed in the lobby.

They were smoking in there,
Short of breath,

And sold Tobacco,
And her husband's death
Was the first I had known
In the world.

They had a sign, and what would I not give
To remember that sign.
German waiters in the
Clipper Room of
The Hotel Atlantic.
A crisp dinner roll,
Jolly intimacy with the Headwaiter,
Or the woman
Who was not a hat-check girl.

One could
Leap down the stairs leap down the landings
One jump to a landing and
Two landings to a floor,
I seem to remember, faster than
The descent of the elevator.
One's lungs,
Ruined by various years of smoking,
Various sadness,
And tobacco lit with no
Celebratory lighter from
The shop with the unquestionably lost sign,
With the kind, that is what she was,
Mismade, misfeatured woman,
With the man who died,
With the fat, German waiters, with the
Elevator man—one had elected
We could not recall his name
No matter how we tried.

II

Nothing away; no, nothing
One could take away,
No more
Than that which had gone on before,
And no other than
That which went before,
In that soft trial to summon up
Wisdom from memory,
Steam from a cold cup.

History Lesson

Leo

I can hardly imagine that if I went for a stroll with any of my well-educated acquaintances (my grandfather is no longer alive) I would hear the following:

"This is where they found Rasputin's body."

"And this is where Napoleon stayed."

Or, "See that little hill? Behind it there's a grove of trees, and that's where Denis Davydov came charging out, when we were already retreating, and inspired our exhausted troops with his astounding deeds . . ."

In Armenia, everyone seems to know such things.

The impression is that history had no beginning in Armenia—it has always existed. In the course of its eternity, it has hallowed every stone, every foot of ground. There is probably no village that was not, in days of old, the capital of an ancient state, no hill around which a decisive battle has not raged, no stone not moistened with blood, and no man to whom this is a matter of indifference.

"Andrei, look. That mountain, way over there—do you see it? And the other one beside it. Right between them is where Prince Andranik met and stopped the Turks, and they turned back."

149

"See that smokestack? And the long building next to it. That's the Central Power Station. Built several years ago. That's where the Molokan sect used to live."

"And this is where Pushkin encountered the cart bearing Griboedov's body . . ."

On and on, without end. I was told these things by taxi drivers and writers, cooks and Party workers, adults and children.

And there was no house where I did not see a certain thick, dark blue book, with three beautiful, confident letters on the cover: LEO. I saw it even in houses where people generally didn't keep books—one or another of the three dark blue volumes by LEO.

Leo was a historian who wrote a three-volume history of Armenia.

As explained to me by specialists, although Leo was a remarkable historian, he was not the best. There have also been scholars more serious than he. But Leo is the most popular. Like our Karamzin or Solovyov.

I ask Russians, "Have you read Karamzin?"

Or, "There was a new edition of Solovyov recently; have you read it?"

We cannot make the excuse that Armenia is small and we're big—that it's easier for them to know their history than for us to know ours. If we multiplied the area of each history by its depth, the volumes, at least, would be equal. And besides, that's not the problem.

I doubt I would find a book by Solovyov in the home of a taxi driver or construction boss. In the homes of writers? One out of ten, at best.

I, for example, have not read him.

But people are always reading Leo. Leo is everywhere. They read as conscientiously as he wrote. He wrote and wrote and knew nothing else in life, wrote from morning to night, every day and all his life. By old age he had gone blind. But he wanted to write his masterpiece, his last. He asked his daughter for pen, paper, and ink.

Blind, he wrote from morning to night.

And finished.

And died.

But the daughter, it turned out, had given the blind man an inkwell without ink, so that he wouldn't make a mess.

He never noticed.

Such is the legend.

Dear God! What did he write?

Connection of the Times

I dream of living this moment. In this moment, by this moment alone. I would then be alive, harmonious, and happy. But I live somewhere between the past and the present of my own life, in hope of a future. I want to eliminate the rupture between past and present, because that rupture makes my life unreal, a nonlife. I keep hoping that through some miraculous effort I will find myself exclusively in the present, never again to lose hold of it, so that my life will once more acquire continuity from birth to death.

Even within a single life, your relationship with time—physical time—is so complicated. And if you add to that your relationship with historical time? And if you extend your segment of personal time along a mental dotted line into the past and the future, beyond your temporal boundaries? If you consider your relationship not with historical time but with the time of history? And if you correlate the time of history with the time of eternity?

This is dizzying, of course. But would it be, if nothing connected you with this abyss? What connects the times? And what connects you with the times?

For ease in handling, we connect the times by means of history. But this is paper twine, temporary packing. If we reject the idea that progress is governed by laws, history is still entertaining as a collection of instructive anecdotes. If we invent governing laws for these anecdotes, they become simply boring.

Besides, is there any such thing as history? Does it exist, objectively? Or is history our accidental relationship to time? And so on. Once I was visited by thoughts like these . . .

. . . I needed to go to Echmiadzin on Sunday. For the Sunday service. My friend did not go with me; he entrusted me to his brother. True, he had his excuses for this, but something makes me think that his customary resistance to revisiting his beloved Meccas was not a factor here. He simply wasn't interested in going to Echmiadzin.

But I absolutely had to go. The Catholicos would be there. The successor to the great coloratura Goar would sing. And, just in general, I wanted to see it.

Hordes of people at the bus stops, all going to Echmiadzin, Echmiadzin. These people, insiders—how many times had they seen and heard it all?—but they were going, and this further convinced me. It was a very intellectual-looking crowd.

A crowd of intellectuals is a type of crowd not often encountered, and rather a surprising sight. Each person believes himself above the laws of the crowd, and yet together they form a crowd. Of all possible crowds, this is the most hypocritical. Though pressed and squeezed on all sides, the intellectual connoisseur nevertheless thinks he still exists in his own personal space. This is very evident on all faces. Their long, tense expressions say that it's not they who are being shoved, not they who are sticking their elbows out, sharply and painfully. Even as he submits to the laws of the crowd, the intellectual believes that he alone, in the mindless crowd, has authentic motives. To see so many masks of detachment on faces a few centimeters from each other is peculiar, to say the least. So I, too, wore an expression of detachment from this astonishing observation, until I was calmed by the sight of a remarkably beautiful young woman who wore around her neck a small, plain gold cross, half buried in a wonderful cleavage. I could look at her for as long as I wished—she had nowhere to hide from me in this stifling crush. She was permitted only to look away from me, for as long as she wished.

So the bus coughed us out into bright space at last, and we hastily disengaged ourselves.

But once we were in the open, the glad cries and handshakes began. "All Yerevan" was here, and everyone knew my friend's brother. I shook hands as his brother's friend (i.e., as his friend, too), and after the handshake I was already a friend of the person whose hand I had just shaken. This, too, might seem peculiar—the degree to which they had all been unacquainted when packed against each other on the bus, and the suddenness with which they joyfully began recognizing each other as soon as they found an opportunity to see themselves a few meters away from their acquaintances. They recognized each other not on drawing close but on drawing apart—or so it appeared. This was confirmed when we all jammed into the cathedral: if you have ten acquaintances in one square meter, you again cease to be acquainted with them. But here you could privately blame concentration and reverence.

Well, I've peopled that space, and now I can tell what I saw. Or, rather, I have a somewhat different task: to tell how I didn't see.

We walked into a park, and the ancient body of a huge cathedral rose before us. For some reason, it looked as if it had been built toward the end of the last century, not sixteen centuries ago. Perhaps its condition had been maintained so assiduously and for so long, the repairs and renovations had been so thorough, that everything had already been replaced; although the contours were the same, a church couldn't be this new—only dishes are this new. Sudden reality: fresh blood on the wall. Blood does have to be fresh—of course. "What's that?" "They kill doves. Bash their heads against the wall." "Why?" "They bring them as sacrifices." "To whom?" "To God." The little boys suddenly became visible, although they'd been milling around the whole time; they had live doves, in bunches, to sell for offerings—and they were normal little boys, looked their age, neither older nor younger. Then we seemed to be elbowing our way into the church . . . The crowd from the bus—but in the church. The service was under way, the ritual. All was decorous, beautiful. What clothes, what faces! At the right, evidently on a platform, the soloist was singing, singing wonderfully, her voice was marvelous, spellbinding, the music was beyond description—great music.

Suddenly it hit me that this was a scene from a bazaar. In one place they were conducting the service, in another place singing, in another place praying, in yet another just gawking. I couldn't understand the proceedings at all. What was wrong? Why, there were no believers! The church was full, jam-packed, you couldn't breathe, your neck and tiptoes ached, but there were no believers. On the right, the philharmonic. On the left, theater. In the rear, curiosity. And only up front, the kneeling vanity of the habitué. Those who had pushed their way forward had already seen their fill—but they had no way back. The service took its normal course, yet its mystery meant nothing to anyone. People studied the clothes and the faces and sniffed the incense, but ten minutes later the clothes were the same, and so were the faces and the fragrance: there was no clear progress. And I . . . Why did I see it this way? What could I be thinking of! For shame.

Now a child started to cry. He, at least, was sincere—he had lost his mother. Such relief in the faces, this was understandable, a child was crying, their souls even stirred within their bodies, and in an understandable way, in sympathy. I would have been glad to cross myself, at least, from shame, but I couldn't remember which side to start on, or how many fingers to use. "The Catholicos! The Catholicos!" At last the crowd came to life—this was the man they'd been waiting for!

There was a movement to get closer, eddies and whirlpools formed, I was pushed to the exit. But I was even glad. Light, air! Divine space. But all those striving toward the goal had mis-calculated: the Catholicos came by a different path, where he wasn't expected. He passed among the gravestones of Catholicoi like himself (he, too, would have a stone here somewhere), and none of the public was there. Only I. He walked through me as if I didn't exist, and stirred up a breeze. I stood petrified, with his breeze blowing on me—and was promptly trampled by the crowd.

I came to in a glade. My friend's brother was by my side, we rejoiced, he introduced me to the soloist, people invited us to sit down on the grass and entertained us so informally, so naturally: Eat, drink! Such excellent people sitting here! While everyone in the church was seeking intellectual diversion and feeling bored, we were eating sacrificial lambs under the open sky: Treat everyone, but don't eat your own sheep . . . Eat, drink, and praise the Lord! We sat on the same ground, under the same sky, shared everything, asked nothing of each other! Peace in our faces, peace in the world. Again we were surrounded by the

miracle of life, of people! Over there, someone had brought a small sheep, so touching, with a red ribbon on his neck, and now they would slaughter him . . . And there in the stony gloom, in a flaming and fatty hell, they would make him into shish kebab, and treat you to it . . . Over there, a woman handed a chicken to some poor little old lady; properly, the woman should have cooked it as a treat for her, but she didn't feel like cooking, and it was all right simply to give the chicken away—let the old lady cook it later for herself . . . The main thing is, give away what's yours and don't eat what you're giving away . . . There I sat, my wine in one hand, my lavash-wrapped* shish kebab in the other, foreign talk all around me—and suddenly I felt good, so childishly good! For an instant, time disappeared, as probably happens only in prayer and in happiness, when the Lord hears . . . And He was certainly casting an eye upon this glade. This would be His Sunday rest.

We had already been invited to a wedding, and also to visit a certain acquaintance of my friend's brother, and also a certain acquaintance of an acquaintance, and also a certain nonacquaintance. The Lord smiled against His will, out of the corner of His mouth . . .

Well, what can you do? What whirlpool of times had set me spinning? The church is sixteen hundred years old, but it has a one-year-old roof; Christianity is two thousand years old, and the sacrifices are ten thousand; the snob entered the cathedral about ten years ago, yet this isn't the first century in which people have observed custom; the newspaper spread under our feast is yesterday's, but the sky above us is eternal; the Catholicos is sixty, I'm thirty—dear God!—the soloist is twenty-five, and there is someone who hasn't even been born and hasn't yet seen the sky!

What different times they come from, the sacrifices and the slogans, the church service and the philharmonic, the snobs and the populace, the buildings and the outbuildings, the text and

---

* Lavash is the first bread, primal bread, the father of bread. Flour and water—so I understand—the crystal of bread. Eternal bread.
"Lavash is bread," my friend says, tearing off a fresh scrap. "Lavash is a plate," he says, putting greens on the lavash. "Lavash is a napkin," he says, wiping his mouth with lavash . . . and eats the napkin.

the singing of it! A hodgepodge, a whirlpool, a rapids of the times, in an instant of time present.

History, in its sequence, is splitting at the seams. Times are connected only by that which has always existed, which does not have time, and which is common to all times. The eternal has no history. History is only for the ephemeral. Biology has a history, but life does not. The state has one, but the people do not. Religion has one, but God does not.

The Book

My friend is an Armenian, and I'm a Russian. We have quite a lot to talk about.

"Oh," my friend said, "if you once show your love, you'll have to answer for it!"

"How do you mean?"

"You'll have to show your love again."

"But if I've ceased to love?"

"Then you've been unfaithful."

"But why?"

"Why did you love before?"

What were we talking about? This . . .

"If I'm an Armenian," he had said, "I'm an Armenian and nothing else. Do I have reason to love any other nation as I love my own? No. But then do I have the right to prefer any one nation to another? Never. You can't be a Judeophile if you're not Jewish, any more than you can be a Judeophobe. Now, you've become an Armenophile, and that's not right."

"I've become an Armenophile? Why do you say that?"

"Because. You've already written one article about me, as an Armenian; you praised me and said only good things. There was no particular reason for you to say them. Later you'll write another article, about this trip. Of course you won't speak ill of the Armenians this time, either; you'll say something good again. Then, the third time, you'll be obligated to love us, to insist on it, so as not to be a traitor. You're already an Armenophile."

"Hmm, yes," I said. "I don't like that."

"I don't either," my friend said. "That's exactly why I've

promised myself never to say anything, either bad or good, about any other nation."

He was right.

But it's too late for me to follow that principle; I can't retract my many words to avoid being unfaithful.

And now I must confess how I fell captive, how I became an Armenophile. I have no right to discuss what I'm about to discuss, just as, having begun, I will have no right not to discuss it. This statement will soon become clear.

. . . One can become an Armenophile without ever noticing when or how it happened. For example, by opening a certain academic book* at any place and reading any page . . .

> In some of the villages the inhabitants were killed, but others were only plundered. Also a substantial number of people, along with their priests, were forcibly converted to Muhammadanism; the churches were turned into mosques.
>
> Most of the villages of Khizan were plundered and subjected to a massacre. Girls and women were raped, and many families were forcibly converted to Muhammadanism. The churches were pillaged, sacred objects were defiled, the priors of the monasteries of Surb Khach and Kamagielya died under dreadful tortures, and the monasteries were pillaged.
>
> The city of Sgerd was subjected to a massacre; the shops and houses were plun . . .

. . . That was the first day of my sojourn in Armenia. I was sitting in the home of my friend's wife's sister, waiting for my friend. I had sampled all the food three times and was listening: my ears were still stopped up after the airplane flight. But my eyes were open. I went out on the balcony.

An unaccustomed scene, which I took to be exotic, unfolded before me. I saw an intersection, and a funeral procession slowly winding across it like a great snake. At home (in my own country) I had long since lost the habit of a ceremonial attitude toward death. Quietly, without darkening my mind, someone bore off my unknown neighbors; I wasn't always aware they had died, any more than I had been aware they were alive.

---

* *The Genocide of the Armenians in the Ottoman Empire: A Collection of Documents and Materials.* The Publishing House of the Academy of Sciences of the Armenian Soviet Socialist Republic, 1966.

In the lead, as if to widen the street and cleanse it of activity (and the street did empty), an open Cadillac convertible glided along with unbearable smoothness and slowness. In it, an impassioned man with a red band on his sleeve stood and directed, like a marshal on parade. Next, in the space he had cleared, came a truck: a scarlet calico platform, an open coffin in the center, and at the corners, on bended knee, four black-suited men, unnaturally straight and stiff (with wreaths in their hands, I think), staring solemnly ahead, apparently not even blinking. Then came such a quantity of Volgas that I lost count.

The force of the impression was not from death, not from grief, not from solemnity—it penetrated from some other, secret passage. That sun, those sweltering black suits, that inexplicably emptied street, that distressing slowness—I felt the world around me thickening, the air and its clarity becoming material objects. In that vitrifying, condensing, white-hot but already congealing world, pain burdened even the movement of the file of vehicles created for speed. They marched soundlessly, on foot, wading, mired in the air, which fell like snow.

Oppressed, I returned to my chair. I picked up the academic book that I had left face down, and looked back a page to see what the topic was . . .

> IX. Bitlis Vilayet. The city of Bitlis was massacred and plundered, together with surrounding villages and districts, which are: (1) Khultik, (2) Muchgoni, (3) Gelnok, (4) . . . (99) Usnus, (100) Kharzet, (101) Agktsop, (102) . . .

What was this? I flipped the pages back . . .

> To Our Supreme Patriarch Mkrtich,
> Most Holy Catholicos of All Armenians—
> Your Holiness, Blessed Hayrik, with tears in our eyes and with sorrowful heart . . .

Who had written this? I turned the page, looked for the signature . . .

> . . . That is our fate and lot. We beg you, we implore you with tears, have pity on the handful of the nation who are yet alive, and if possible do not refuse to cast a handful of water on the fire consuming them.
>
> —Vardapet Hakobyan

I skipped to the end of the book and again opened it "anywhere" . . .

The policy prescribed on this point by the censorship guide, published early in 1917 by the censorship department of the military press, was stated as follows:

"As for the atrocities on the Armenians, one may say the following: not only must these issues, which concern internal administration, not threaten our friendly relations with Turkey, but at the present difficult moment it is also essential that we refrain from even examining them. Therefore it is our duty to maintain silence. Later, if foreign countries directly accuse Germany of complicity, we shall have to discuss this issue, but with the greatest care and restraint, always stating that the Turks were dangerously provoked by the Armenians. It is best to maintain silence on the Armenian question."

What was this from? I turned the page . . . "Joseph Marquard, on the Plan to Exterminate the Western Armenians." Who was Marquard?

A throttled sensation akin to impatience again picked me up and led me out to the balcony. A new funeral, just as long and magnificent as the first, was crossing the intersection . . .

Here my device betrays me, although that is exactly the way it happened: my first day, sunny and deaf, I wait for my friend and see a funeral and open a book . . . But by now I don't believe in this sequence and can't bear it.

All this did happen then, but when I wrote about it later I no longer had the book at hand. After writing that the book could be opened anywhere, I left a blank page. My story was finished, but near the beginning of the manuscript, just about here, the skipped page was still white: that book had proved to be as hard to obtain as the Bible.

I am writing these lines at the Leningrad Public Library on February 18, 1969, in order to fill in the blank.

I'm sitting in the library, holding that book in my hands again at last. There are five hundred pages in it. I have two hours, and I realize that I will not succeed in selecting the most characteristic, vivid, and impressive passages. And realize, too, that even if I could, it would be false. I resolve to repeat my experiment. I open the volume anywhere, crack it in the middle . . .

Of the 18,000 Armenians exiled from Kharberd and Sebastia, 350 women and children reached Aleppo; of the 19,000 exiled from Arzrum, only 11 people. Muslims who have traveled this road relate that the route is impassable because of the numerous corpses lying there poisoning the air with their stench.

This from the travel notes of a German, an eyewitness to the events in Kilikia.

I turn back a hundred pages.

Madame Doti-Vili writes: "The Turks do not kill the men immediately, and as they welter in blood their wives are raped before their very eyes." Because it is not enough for them to kill. They maim, they torture. "We hear bloodcurdling cries," writes Sister Maria-Sophia, "the howl of unfortunates whose stomachs are being ripped open, who are undergoing torture."

Many witnesses relate that Armenians were bound by both feet, head down, like carcasses at a slaughterhouse, and split with an ax. Others were tied to a wooden bed, which was then set afire; many were nailed alive to the floor, to doors, to tables.

Monstrous pranks are also carried out, sinister games. They seize and bind an Armenian, and on his motionless lap they saw up his children or hack them to pieces. Father Benois, of the French missionaries, reports acts of yet another kind: "The executioners juggled with recently severed heads, and even as the parents watched they tossed up little children and caught them on the tips of their cutlasses."

The tortures are sometimes crude, sometimes skillfully refined. Some victims undergo a whole series of tortures, conducted with flawless art in order to prolong the martyr's life and thereby prolong the amusement: they maim them slowly, at a measured pace, pulling out their nails, breaking their fingers, tattooing the body with a red-hot iron; they remove the scalp from the skull, and toward the end make it into porridge, which they toss to feed the dogs. They break the bones of some, little by little; they crucify others, or set them on fire like a torch. Crowds of people gather around, enjoying the spectacle and applauding the victim's every movement.

At times these are terrifying abominations, the orgies of sadists. They cut off an Armenian's limbs, then compel him to chew pieces of his own flesh. They choke women to death by forcing into their mouths the flesh of their own children. They rip open the stomachs of others and stuff into the gaping wound the quartered body of the child whom they recently carried in their arms.

I have opened this book in four places. I can't do it again.
I feel like a murderer copying these words, and I'm almost
peering over my shoulder to be sure no one's looking. About
a hundred people are sitting here, and no one knows what I'm
doing. They're all quietly writing doctoral dissertations. I'm sure
I'm engaged in the most terrible work in this building. I very
much want them to believe me: I really didn't select anything,
I merely opened the book in four places, any way it opened. I
can swear any oath that this is not a device, it's really true. The
book has another five hundred pages that I haven't read.

I ran out of black ink when I opened the book the fourth
time, and I am forced to write in red pencil. This is neither
manipulation nor symbol—it's chance—but my pages are red.

There is enough of everything in this world. If we think that
something doesn't exist, that it can't exist, that it's impossible—
then it exists. If we but think it, it already exists.

This world has everything, and for everything there is a
place.

Everything finds room.

I won't open the book again, I'm not going to read it. Back
then in Armenia, I think, on my first day, I opened the book to
the very passage I last quoted. And down below, a red funeral
was passing by . . . It no longer seemed exotic to me: a different
sun, a different death, a different attitude toward death.

And now, while I rest and calm down a bit, having resolved
not to look into this book again, I can glance at the table of
contents before handing the book back to the librarian:

1. The Massacre of the Armenians under Sultan Abdul Gamid
   (1876–1908).
2. The Mass Slaughter of the Armenians by the Young Turks
   (1909–1918).

That is the entire table of contents. How neatly 1908 fits
next to 1909! As the last page of the first volume fits next to the
first page of the second. A two-volume edition. Early works—
the first volume. Posthumous publications—the second.

And a foreword, too . . .

What was the total number of Armenians who perished?
A detailed study of the question leaves no doubt that in the
years of Sultan Abdul Gamid's supremacy about three hundred

thousand people died; in the period of the Young Turks' rule, half a million. Approximately eight hundred thousand refugees found asylum in the Caucasus, the Arabian East, and other countries. It is instructive that if, in the 1870s, more than three million Armenians lived in Western Armenia and throughout the Turkish Empire generally, in 1918 there were only two hundred thousand.*

The Russian for "massacre" is *reznyá*. But my friend says *réznya*, with the accent on the root, which is from the verb "to cut." I simply cannot get his pronunciation out of my mind. As though *reznyá* is just people massacring each other somewhere . . . but "*réznya*" is when they're cutting *you*. The taste of your own flesh in your mouth.

History With Geography

Y ou've already seen this, of course," said the history teacher (my friend's wife's sister), taking from the shelf a book as flat as lavash. "What! You *haven't?*"
We sat down on the couch and cracked the atlas in half: one half covered her lap, the other mine. I hadn't seen this kind of atlas since the good old days when I used to cock my head to one side and stick my tongue out as I colored Kievan Russia red.

I looked at these colored maps and caught a melancholy whiff of homework assignments.

The maps are mute for me, Armenian names in the Armenian language. Blue—that's the sea. Armenia is sometimes yellow, sometimes green, depending on the epoch. I am bombarded with names of conquering Armenians and conquerors of Armenia—a forest of centuries and names. My own history seems to me to be sparsely wooded, because, where we have our antiquity in the seventeenth century, theirs is in the seventh, and where we

---

* After the genocide, half of all Armenians were living abroad as émigrés. But Armenians do not accept the word *émigré*. For them, the word is an insult. To leave your country because of political convictions, or in search of a better life, is one thing; but it's another to save your wife and children from rape and the curved knife.

have the seventh, they have the third B.C. We don't even have the third.

Here, green and round, Armenia extends to three seas. Here, to two. Here, to one. And here—not even to one. So swiftly does Armenia diminish from the first map to the last, always remaining a generally round state, that if you riffle quickly through the atlas, it's a movie: it captures the fall of a huge round stone from the altitude of millennia. The stone disappears into the deep, diminishing to a point. But if you riffle the pages from the end to the beginning, it's as if a small pebble has fallen into the water, and historical circles are spreading across the water, ever wider and wider.

My friend came in and saw.

"Ah," he said, "the atlas . . ."

He sat down on the couch, took the atlas on his lap, opened it . . . And disappeared. Became absorbed in it—literally. With each turn or blow of the page he sank into his history up to his knees, his waist, his chest. He went all the way under. Suddenly he surfaced and looked up at me from the depths with faraway eyes, as if holding his head high out of the water. His voice barely reaching me, he shouted: "What I don't like in Armenians, sometimes, is their bellicosity."

"What? What?" I shouted, into the depths of his well. My voice drifted down and down but seemed never to reach bottom.

Again my friend bent and looked for something at the bottom. He must have lost a ring . . .

Finally he climbed out on the surface of modernity. Before him lay the most recent map, today's Armenia. He drew a line with his fingernail, cutting off a narrow little strip on the east.*

"That will be nice. A nice round republic . . ."

I no longer knew whether to shout to him deep down or high up. I smiled foolishly.

The Armenians are a warlike people. For several thousand years they conquered; for several thousand years they were conquered. Their latest war is the war for their own history. Of

---

* An inside joke. The "strip on the east" divides the Nakhichevan A.S.S.R. from the Nagorno-Karabakh Autonomous Region. Both these regions, with their predominantly Armenian populations, are part of Azerbaijan.

this atlas—whose publication, it turns out, was also a struggle—and of the collection of materials on genocide especially, and of the defeat of Klimov, they speak with pride and pain, as one speaks of victory.

. . . My friend's brother came in. The taciturn younger brother. We had been waiting for him to arrive with news: he had taken his wife to the maternity hospital. He walked silently to the couch, lifted the atlas like a burden, and silently sank into it.

He looked through the telescope of his history. He trained reverse binoculars on his country, and there, in the improbable depth, at the bottom, shone the ring of Lake Sevan, and perhaps his future son.

Translated by Susan Brownsberger

Die Silbergäule.
A-N-N-A
dada
Schwitters. 1919.
Kurt Schwitters.
ANNA BLUME.
Dichtungen.
Paul Steegemann, Verlag, Hannover.

The Onion:
Merzpoem 8
(1919)

The day that I was to be slaughtered was a very busy day. (Don't be afraid, just keep the faith!) The king was set, his two attendants waiting. The butcher had been asked to come at six thirty; it was a quarter to seven and I gave the orders myself to start the customary preparations. We had picked a spacious hall so that the many spectators could watch the show in comfort. The telephone was near to hand. The doctor was living in the house next door and was on call in the event that any spectators passed out. (A keepsake from your confirmation.) Two powerful tackle blocks were hanging from the ceiling, to crank me up should they decide to gut me. Four strong laborers were there to lend a hand: erstwhile Russian prisoners of war, bigboned and hardy handsome (Journal for Real Estate and Household Management). Two well scrubbed maids were also there on call, two super-scrubbdup farmgirls. It was a real kick thinking that these two young girls would whisk my blood and wash and salt my innards.

The hall had been swept and washed. I had two long, cleanscraped tables set up along one of the walls, on which stood several bowls, knives, forks. Now I had a washbasin, water and a towel brought in, also some dish detergent (sunlight). Anna and Emma, the two maids, brought out a bucket and a whisk. Knowing that you'll be butchered in ten minutes gives you a funny kind of feeling. (The sacrifices of a mother's love.) Until then I had never in my life been butchered. It takes a lot of growing up. Anyway, once the potatoes have been taken out and once the oats are cut, that's when things can turn real bad. And so far we haven't had a decent summer anyway. (Faith, love, great expectations.) (Ducks are goosing in the meadow.) Every little detail taken care of.

And now the princess was arriving. She had a short white dress on, which had got a little twisted, but that only made her sexier. Because the church tower is extremely steep. Dedicated to Lenzesflur in friendship. Jumping and kicking, the king's daughter and her delicate short legs. I love these delicate kicking jumpingkingsdaughterslittlelegs. Tail waggles sour cream. She herself stood inkwell to my face and whistleclean asked white embroidery. "Are you going to be butchered now today?" Hot fishing knives shot blood. I lowered purple eyes, made happy by her greeting. "How beautiful you are, you Elvis Broomsticker, gorgeous hunk!" she said red lips veins do boil blood, happy trails! pert sharplythreaded nose: "I'm bringing you last greetings from the world. Thou should become a nun! (May my house be thy world.) (Leather without a head.) Tooled leather set to navel measure. These days you're really in a hurry, getting things lined up for this important day. (Peace be with you.) How you do grow up — grow ripe — grow overripe! How joyfully you look at your own ripeness! May it always bring you joy! How lucky that the weather stayed good for your butchering, that way the butcher can get here by bike." (Authentic Brussels handiwork.) Good Health is Fortune's Gift. "Please, little princess, will you let me phone. It is half past six already and the butcher isn't here." "Hello! Is this the butcher speaking? The spectators are starting to get restless, how come you aren't here yet?" (From here yet to eternity!) "Have them start up the festivities without me. I just kebabd my sister on the church spire, like a weathervane. And as you know the church spire is very steep and up above it a fish spikes in whipair. The lightning rod was very rusty and tough to jab it through my sister's belly. But fish spikes blank in whipstink. Have them start up the formalities without me!"

I let the king be called. "Majesty, I do commend my

lovely form unto thine hands. May your majesty take command over my corpse-to-be!'' (20 cents per millimeter line per six column page.) The king waved back. (Fortuna Grindstones.) The two attendants in black frockcoats, gloves, top hats, and black neckties took their places at the king's two sides. A black dog flew past, cawing. Again the king waved. The four Russians plus Anna and Emma got ready to lend a hand. The king waved again. The attendants approached me, stood in front of me, and asked about my last wishes. (Look up at that star!) I requested the Princess to sing the great workers song and then kiss me. (Acephalous necks, leather jerky.) A lady from the royal entourage swooned and fell down on the floor. The doctor was summoned. Strong does whip inward. The princess then sang:

"Workers grind organs
C-sharp D
D-sharp E-flat
E-sharp E
Thou thine thy thee,''

the very great workers song. Lanternstake does grind organ do kiss the broad skirts wave white points a kiss. To sling arms broad skirts do wave neck points warm tubes do smooth slim fish carps, carps, carps. (Prière de fermer la porte.) Please, please close the door, Thou, Thou, Thou! For I love thee so very! (This world with its sinfuls.)

Now butcher me!

The king waves again and the butcher drives forth. The house has gone mute. Pro patria est, dum ludere videmur (blue-red-yellow girls club). (Smoking Forbidden. Even unlit cigars held in hand are prohibited.) Two laborers who took his bike away. (National welfare tax.) A laborer brings out a cudgel, big lemonpale balloon. (Hold on to what you've got!) The butcher wears a blue striped apron flutter cloth. (Beet Sugar Baby.) October bends down ceremonies enemies attendants. — Scat! — Me hedgehog! — Butcher is leaning back, head tilted, cudgel raised behind. (The greatest gift, the fairest joy, is home-sweethome domestic bliss!) The butcher springs forward (That's love for you), swings cudgel down down down hard hard hard, does whip inward down hard hard hard very very very very.

My skull caved in.

Now I had to fall to pieces, so I fell, I fell to pieces, fell, fell flat. Aaaaa aaaaa aaaaa aaaaa b. (Applause from all the benches.)

So what's the story now? They strapped my arms and legs to winches, winches winch me up. Sinking slings flat to pieces slantily spread out. (Calling all blue- and white-collar workers.) They stabbed me in the side. Blood rinseth bucket blue stream red thick whip. Turns maids a whisk to pieces break upon the wheel railroad machines do Emma Anna whisk. (In all innocence you 'ave hallowed thy heart for the Holy Alliance t'day!) The king demanded a drink. Blue singed flame murder far gone far gone. Hollow burns stomach flame sulfur blood. Since which time the king is beardless. Be true to your duty, be true. (Presented by the Editorial Committee.) For everything has its own science. (Amplificatores, Advisory Council for Capitalist Reconstruction, Berlin.)

They were going to gut me. (Newest Mocha Bonbons, A Novelty.) Transfers drive knife do slit tremble intestines. (Peace Commodities.) It was a garden restaurant well worth the visit. I felt a thousand joys o savior morning twenty. The creature bred in the glass house blossomed only for three lustra. (Roaring cheers.) Mooncalf inward glows soft pulled intestines fat pain soft swooned. (All this for the Red Army.) Clean, clean, be clean, girls, clean when washing, so that nothing will get burnt. (May God preserve you.) (God preserve you.)

Flame hot, flame hot! Earthworms inward played soft in my belly, it tickled so slight. The king lusted my eyes. O fetch me, king's daughter, the eyes of Johanan. (Thou art moving this day from the House of thy Father.) Round spheres inward smooth slime they sprang from the eyes the soft hands fully towards. With a plate, knife and fork they served eyes. (Old warriors hard of hearing and totally deaf get facts and advice at no charge.) Smooth slimed oysters eyes sink stomach heavy. Children under twelve admitted only with parental supervision, children under eight must be led through by hand. (Admission fifty pfennigs, minimum one mark.)

"Poison!" screamed the king while rolling on the floor. (To populate the earth, the cradle proves its worth.) "Sweet dreams, but in the meantime I've been poisoned." (31 days in August, daytime growing shorter by one hour 56 minutes.) You bet,

it really sucks. "O Lord I build my house on thee, I raise my hands!" Two mushrooms grew eyes stem smooth tubers milk skyhigh and drilled holes two into king's belly. Stemeyed eyes did eye. Mute scared a king chalk. Princess's heart was beating something awful. (Acetylene eliminates the smell of bodily secretions.) She felt such wondrous pity for her father. The doctor was summoned fussing with the holes in the king's belly. (Veritas Vincit — Anna Blossom in the starring role.) Then the old king passed out. Fear peaks silver tendrils stone to stone. The princess waved and ordered them to put me back together. (That's how one cleans, dusts, washes, steams, and dries bed feathers.)

They started to put me back together. With a little gentle pressure they pushed my eyes back in their sockets. (Have no fear: faith, love, great expectations are thy stars.) Then they gathered up my innards. Happily nothing had been cooked yet, and nothing had been ground up for sausages. (Vaincu, mais non dompté.) And still one is pleased to see another pretty autumn. Because of my inner magnetic currents, my inner parts (once they were stuffed inside) began to jerk spasmodically and then stuck hard and fast together. (The art of happy days in marriage.) When setting the intestines back in place, certain problems had to be worked out, that was how much they'd gotten intermeshed. (Saint Florian Moves into German Theater. Comic Extravaganzas Nightly.) But I noticed what was going on, directed my magnetic currents hither and thither, to and fro, one two one two one two one the tone to uproot mote in eye. I pushed and pulled magnetically on the intestines, until they lay in their accustomed places. My knowledge of man's inner nature was a boon to me. (After a one-year tryout, lands a permanent position as a Prussian state official.) Jawohl! Meanwhile my solid parts had been put back together; the only thing still missing was the blood. (Bordens sweet milkchocolate.) The maids held the bowl with blood under the stabwound in my side and whisked it in the opposite direction. The king gave an audible groan. Drawn by my magnetic currents a thick jet of blood rose up from its red surface and slammed into my stabwound. (Mustn't tell the girls what every woman has to know.) Slowly my veins filled up, my heart was full, the inner parts began to take in blood. But the heart didn't move, I was still dead. (Fresh paint!) With his knife the butcher touched the stabwound in my side, plunged the blade in deep, pulled the knife out — and the wound closed up. (Detach and mail to the above address.) That's why every woman should inform herself, at least once she has gotten married. Once again now all my parts were back together, there were just a few small holes where bits of flesh were still adhering to the knives. The desire and the need for it are clearly present, although the time ain't right. Besides there was a lack of blood, because the king had drunk it. (For the ideals of socialism.) Ever since I've been a tad anemic. Take the cage home with you and buy yourself a bird. The lowered winches winched down tackle blocks. Now I had to straighten up, I thought, and so I straightened up; quickly at first and then slower and slower until I was standing up straight. (My heart and maw were red and raw.) A slip of a girl grew up in Burgundy, for I am only a squaw. O child, be mindful of whither you move! Be faithful and true! Remain faithful, o child, step forward in life, don't be shy. (Vote socialist too!) Then the two attendants took places beside me, ceremoniously grasping my hands. (Prescriptions filled for all health plans.) Beautiful childhood is over and past, the struggle for life has now started at last. And I was dying to know how they would bring me back to life. It is strictly forbidden to touch any object in this collection. I was dizzy. (Strindberg to gradually unroot Stramm.) Our good old teacher liked to spice his teaching up with little jokes, and there was nothing wrong with that. (Sungazing.) I don't believe in anything. (Trumpet jamboree.) You got it right! In this most trying of times an appeal to all Bible-thumping evangelical woman preachers! (What every man should know about pregnancy and childbirth!) Your maw's a saw. (Old Doctor Sunshine.)

The butcher grabbed his cudgel again (the tragedy of being human), stood it in front of me (the behavior of men during pregnancy), and gently rested it on my split skull. (Rudolf Bauer's a genuine artist.) Anna Blossom abideth lilac-blue roses does shoot sting hole stinkhole. (Ripe for the plucking, united at heart.) Incomplete information misses the mark. Then the butcher jumped backwards with a godawful jerk. (The major is and will always be a "gentleman," although he's also a twit.)

That woman has to know it all. There was a godawful crash when the cudgel drew back from my head. A book designed especially for women offers this rare chance. Table of Contents: 1. How to win love. — 2. The tamed shrew. — 3. What girls go for in a man. — 4. Something about kissing. — 5. How to make a good impression. — 6. How to deal with a rejection. — 7. Is shyness justified in marriage? — 8. The roots of abstinence. — 9. Older views. — 10. How to practice moderation. — 11. A good piece of advice. — 12. Is love blind? — 13. How to recognize true love. — 14. The man's past. — 15. The most intimate intimacy. — 16. The new faith. — 17. The dark star. The butcher jumped backwards into his original stance. (He shall be your Lord.) But the company's true pillar remains forever without guile. (Jamais embrassé.) The bits and pieces of my skull flew back together, I was just about complete again. (Sweet moment.) Fritters you don't like and gherkins are too fat for you. And anyway the theater only exists for people who aren't people anyway. The book is richly illustrated and will be sent you on receipt of payment due.

It felt really strange to be alive again. Seltzer water sails light up perfume Maria. I felt I had to pose a little, and so I posed a little. (Just then the king died.) With a grand flourish I walked up to the king's daughter and offered her my hand in silence. (Kiss me!) The king's daughter fell on her pretty bony knees in front of me. (From back in downhome country.) The doctor meanwhile fletcherized pork knuckles. Help wanted ads continued in the supplement. She begged me urgently to save her father. (Happiness inside the haidehaus.) I knew I couldn't stay goodnatured in this instance, not when anyone can spot a dummy by his easy nature. (Anna Blossom hanging tough.) (Old age real scary.) I told her: "Your father the king, the king will stay dead." (Razor strap from seal pelts.) Then the doctor swooned. I had them set two candles made of yellow wax into the king's belly, then had the candles lit. (Payment in stamps.) When the flame flared through the holes in the king's belly, the king exploded. But the people offered me a last hurrah. (Socialism = Work.)

Translated by Pierre Joris and Jerome Rothenberg

Final W.

You who first gave me shelter
Kept count with the pressure of your own heart.
Now you watch worry shale away that pulse.
The arm of death becomes your cradle;
Your voice begins its final caution:
"Whatever circles the devil's back
Buckles under his stomach.
Whatever goes over his shoulders
Carries the weight of his desire."

A butcher's silence falls.
A particular white annoys the ground.
This is the house of winter;
It gathers the scent of your age.
I pursue the falling dust of sleep
With a vicious domestic hand.
I finger the braille facts of your dying;
Love becomes a gesture beyond cleaning.

DOMINIQUE WADE

Trophies of War

[Angola]

BACKGROUND

P.R.A. / People's Republic of Angola / Southern Africa /
Capital: Luanda / Former Portuguese colony / Five centuries
of colonization / War of independence: February 4, 1961-
November 11, 1975 / Independence: November 11, 1975 /
Fourteen years of anticolonialist guerilla warfare /
Followed by: Fourteen years of civil war / Rebel movement:
UNITA, União Para a Independencia Total de Angola /
Supported by: the Republic of South Africa, the United
States of America / Controls: the southeast, the east, the
northeast / MPLA: Movimento Popular de Liberação de Angola:
party in power / Supported until 1988 by: U.S.S.R., Cuba /
Defense effort until 1988: according to estimates in
diplomatic circles, 70% of the state's resources / Economic
potential: a continental plateau teeming with petroleum,
diamonds, copper, iron, phosphate, uranium . . . / Diamonds
are gathered in the rivers / Soldiers have seen sources of
pure mercury, mountains of quartz in the open air / Climate:
tropical / On the cool, high plateaus, everything grows,
even grapes and strawberries / The coast: one of the world's
richest in fish / Economic situation: catastrophic /
Inflation until 1989: One bottle of whiskey, 10,000 kwanzas;
monthly salary of an office worker, 15,000 kwanzas / Black
market: immeasurable / Official exchange rate in 1989: 1
dollar = 30 kwanzas / Unofficial rate: 1 dollar = 3000
kwanzas / Growth through 1988: scandalous / 1986: the
Pentagon for the first time agrees to provide sophisticated
arms to guerillas it supports: Afghanistan, Nicaragua,
Angola, Khmers Rouges . . . / The CIA's delivery of the
famous "Stinger" surface-to-air missile, electronic bazooka,
portable anti-aircraft missiles capable of reaching a flying
airplane at an altitude of 4 to 5 miles / Guidance system:
self-guiding, infrared / Justification: the U.S.S.R.'s
delivery to Angola and Afghanistan of MIG 21 and MIG 23
fighter planes and MI 24 helicopters—flying armored tanks
with cannon and rocket launchers / Carrying: 10 commandos /
Official slogans: "Every citizen must feel like a soldier,"
"An economy to support the war, a war to support the

economy" / Battle of Cuito Cuanavale, February–April 1988: brutal clash in Angolan territory between the South African Defense Force and UNITA on one side and governmental forces, SWAPO, and Cuban troops on the other / Neither side is really victorious: confirmation that military resolution of the situation is impossible / December 22, 1988: tripartate peace treaties are signed / Between: South Africa, Angola, Cuba / Administered by the Americans and supervised by the UN / January 1989: under flags faded by the sun, the first of the 50,000 "barbudos cubanos" leave with their arms under UN control / The Namibian refugees from SWAPO regain their entire territory by air power / They will vote for independence / Independence of Namibia: April 1990 /

South Africa withdraws its troops from Namibia / UNITA suffers greatly with the end of South African support / At the request of UNITA, the U.S. Congress votes 30 million dollars in aid at the beginning of 1991 / (Off the record, the CIA would have offered twice as much) / Jonas Savimbi moves his troops to the north of Angola: there he benefits from Zairean complicity and the support of the large U.S. military base in Zaire, the Camina base / Excluded from the peace treaties, incapable of winning a battle by conventional means, Jonas Savimbi revives the art of sabotage and atrocities /

Today, after an overdue ceasefire, free elections are taking place /

The economic situation remains catastrophic: in a self-proclaimed socialist country, only the large foreign companies, generators of juicy contracts and hard currencies, have been spared /

Here, as elsewhere, the path of unopposed capitalism seems irreversibly enticing /

                                        —Dominique Wade

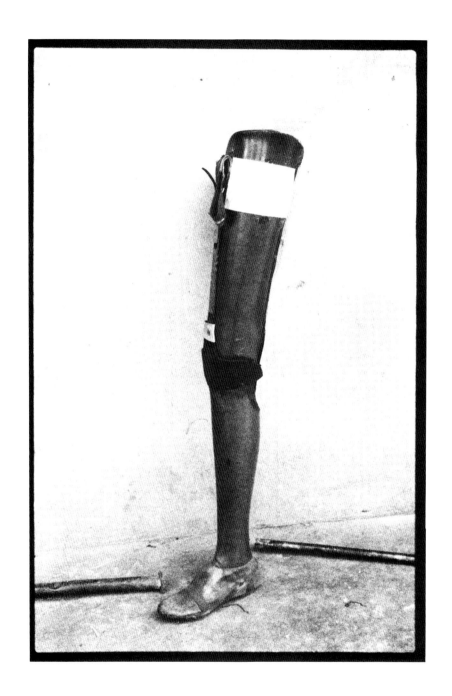

Trophies of War [Angola]

p. 177   **Cuito Cuanavale:** South African F.N. machine gun (Belgian-made)

p. 180   **Cuito Bié:** Prosthetic leg at a physiotherapy clinic. One hundred thousand people lost arms or legs to antipersonnel mines

p. 181   **Cuito Cuanavale:** Armored S.A.D.F. troop carrier, "Hippo"

p. 182   **The Phantom Dagger That Saved Captain Jacinto Tchipa's Life:** A war prize, taken from a U.S. M16, which Tchipa carried on his hip

p. 183   **Captain Tchipa:** A FAPLA officer, blinded during an S.A.D.F. commando ambush on Angolan territory

p. 184   **Cabinda:** Trophy display including the kit of a South African Captain, Wayne Petrus, shot down during a raid on Gulf Oil Company installations

p. 185   **Iocola Damba:** Trophy display including photographs of torture scene, decapitation, Western mercenaries. "Iocola Damba" is the *nom de guerre* of a Portuguese militiaman, hand-embroidered on his beret

p. 186   **Paulinho:** A FAPLA soldier

p. 187   **Paulinho:** Portrait

p. 188   **Soviet Star:** Armored vehicle

p. 189   **Protée:** Trophy display including kit and photograph of a dead South African pilot, shot down in his Mirage fighter plane

p. 190   **Ruacana:** South African shortwave radio, manufactured in Japan

Cuito Cuanavale and **Ruacana** are S.A.D.F. or Angolan and Cuban names for battles. **Cabinda** and **Protée** are names of S.A.D.F. commando missions in Angolan territory.

Natural Life

I
t was September 26, 1981. The man I had traveled to meet had once been a prominent professional boxer. Now he was six years into a life sentence at the maximum-security Louisiana State Penitentiary in Angola, Louisiana.

A tall, acne-blistered guard made small talk. His black uniform rustled synthetically as he showed me along the outdoor walkway toward Cuda tier, an isolated one-story compound at the far end of the yard in Camp J, Angola's special outpost for problem prisoners. The guard seemed to have the mistaken idea that I was someone officially important, possibly a journalist, and he asked deferential, countrified questions that vaguely pertained to documentary reporting and to publishing a book. I looked at his pale, suffering skin and answered in a way that didn't directly correct his false impression of me. My omission probably led him to pass on the same mistake to the caretaker at Cuda, who eventually peered out from behind the steel door that the guard rapped on. The caretaker, who I guessed was a trusty, wore deeply wrinkled clothes, and he looked groggy— either drugged or as if we had roused him. They conferred for a moment, the caretaker nodding vacantly. Then, to my surprise, the guard obligingly waved me inside and walked away.

From the glare of the open walkway, I stepped uncertainly into a dim, barren room. The only light came from a wrenched gooseneck lamp. Drawn up to a metal desk littered with the remains of a meal stood a grimy stuffed chair. It was like a nest—crammed with newspapers and copies of *Penthouse,* mashed pillows, and a visibly greasy transistor radio.

After the caretaker had locked himself and me in, he straightened slowly, as if he had back trouble, and asked without interest "which of 'em" I was supposed to see. I had just noticed, next to the desk, a door with a barred window in it. When I told him whom I had come to visit, he scuffed over to this door and shouted an order I couldn't understand through the bars. Then, groping among the keys on his ring, he set about opening the lock beneath the window.

Beyond the windowed door was a second door, all bars. These yielded a full view of a corridor and a young man partly wrapped in a towel and wearing a shower cap. Taking short, precise steps, he came toward us from the entrance to the showers at the far end of the corridor. Cement block enclosed the corridor to the right; ventilation slats near the ceiling let in fanlike stripes of light. To the left, I made out a row of about a dozen cells. The caretaker shouted impatiently at the man in the towel while working a switch that caused the door to the prisoner's cell to slide open, then to shut behind him. The caretaker swiped at another switch with the edge of his hand. The bars before us shuddered and snicked open.

"He down there. About on the end."

I waited for the man to lead the way. When he didn't move, it struck me in a rush that he assumed I had clearance to be anywhere in the prison.

On crepe soles, I stepped silently into the corridor, trying to move with a confidence I've never felt.

The prisoners were sleeping. Or seemed to be. Numbly I moved through the striped light, and through a sodden moist smell I'll never be able to name, or forget. In each toilet-dominated cell, a man's prone form lay on a steel bunk suspended on two chains. Not one of the prisoners was white, and each lay turned toward the wall, drawn in to himself—except for the one who had come from the shower. He stood, penis semierect, clenching the balled-up hems of the towel now yoked across the back of his neck.

The prisoner in the next cell snored. I saw dingy undershorts and a huge man's massive bulk.

And then I saw Alvin.

It wasn't the posters or the snapshots or the sports-page photographs I had pored over that made me know him at once: he didn't look like *them* anymore. Unlike the other prisoners in Cuda, he lay with his head at the foot of his bunk, facing the bars, jaw cradled in the crook of his arm. As I stepped silently into view, filling the space he had been gazing across, he peered up, big-eyed. Despite the scar tissue and his now permanently sagging right brow—caused, if family rumor could be believed, by spooked guards who had beaten him with bats— I saw his father, Collis Phillips, stamped unmistakably in the open expression in and around his eyes. It was a look in which curiosity replaced caution. When I stayed where I was, making it clear that he was why I was there, the look vanished and he recoiled toward the wall.

After I had begun to talk—about what, I don't recall—he finally roused himself, rose deliberately, and took the single step from his bunk to the bars. It seemed to disturb and confuse him when, without my willing it, giddy nervous energy caused me to reach into his cell.

After pausing and looking at it squarely, he took my hand and, in odd social compliance, shook it: a fighter's limp grip, protective of his own knuckles.

For a moment I just looked at him.

• • •

Just about anyone who diligently read the New Orleans newspaper could, at that time, have known almost as much about Alvin Phillips as I did. In June, for example, the *Times-Picayune* had run a feature article by Alan Citron, a news reporter who had won awards for his writing about state institutions. His article summarized Alvin's boxing career, his drug addiction, and his imprisonment for selling a small amount of heroin to an undercover agent. All of this I knew from sports pages and from conversations in passing with Collis. I hadn't known—until Citron reported it—that Alvin was serving a life sentence. Nor did I then know—and the report hadn't mentioned this—that the sentence was for "natural life," which meant Alvin was ineligible for parole. Nor that this sentence was based on his only adult conviction.

The article contained other startling information, too: that Alvin refused to perform required work in Angola; that in his five years there, he had been written up for sixty-eight violations of prison rules; that for an indeterminate stretch of time he had been confined to a solitary cell for twenty-three hours of each day, apparently as a disciplinary measure; and that he had mutilated himself twice with a razor and once, more recently, by pouring laundry bleach into his eyes.

For me the most intriguing passage in Alan Citron's report was rendered in Alvin's own words: "Me, I don't know anything. I was just a lot of front street action. I got disgusted with the pressure of life. Working, fighting, kids. What are you going to do about anything? Drugs were escapism. I thought it was smarter to sell than to buy. Now I've turned myself off. I could really turn myself on, you know, with booze and all that, but that's no good. My hook stinks now, but goddam. Other fighters keep themselves mad. I couldn't keep myself mad."

• • •

His career began almost by accident in the mid-sixties. His father, my friend Collis, was then running Vince Arnona's gym in the warehouse district on Tchoupitoulas Street. Alvin worked not far away at Woodward, Wight & Co. In the afternoons, after work, unless Collis had a ride, Alvin would stop by the gym to wait to go home with him on the bus.

The star of the Tchoupitoulas gym was Jerry Pellegrini, a white welterweight and middleweight contender whose training Collis supervised for Arnona. Pellegrini hit hard, and it was difficult to keep him in sparring partners. One afternoon when no one else was available, Collis asked Alvin to go up into the ring and give Pellegrini some work. Alvin took off his shoes and, in his first formal sparring session, boxed in jeans and bare feet.

In "A Champ at Ringside," a story and interview that

appeared in the *Times Picayune* the morning of the second of
Alvin's locally celebrated fights with the contender Tony Licata,
the New Orleans sports journalist Waddell Summers quoted
Collis's description of his son's start, an account that was similar
to others I had heard from various people who had known Alvin.
"Well, Alvin used to come by the gym to see me," Collis told
Summers. "So one day Alvin got in the ring and we just told
him to move a lot. Alvin was fast but didn't know anything about
boxing. Jerry didn't try to hurt him. Actually, Jerry taught him a
lot. Jerry is a good kid, a fine young man . . . Alvin learned fast.
Jerry gave him ideas and pretty soon there was Alvin, starting
to box pro in his first four-rounder.

"It really surprised me when Alvin decided to be a boxer. He
could have been boxing at fifteen or sixteen. But I never enticed
any of my sons to be fighters. It's such hard work and such a long
road to travel. I advised all my kids to get an education. I don't
want to stand in the way of my kids. I told Alvin if he wanted
to fight, I would help him. I didn't ask him to be a fighter, but
I would never try to stop my son from doing what he's doing.
Two of my sons, Collis Jr. and Jerry, fought some amateur, but
Alvin never did. I guess Alvin has natural talent—that's the only
thing I can call it."

In his first fight, at the age of twenty-five, Alvin didn't look
so much like a natural. He fought on the undercard of a Jerry
Pellegrini show and lost a four-round decision to an opponent
named Preston Price. Collis told me he "looked like he had a
little stage fright" that night; he "didn't stay busy enough" and
"let the decision git away from him." Collis said he "got on him
heavy" about it afterward.

After that, Alvin won fifteen straight, all at the Municipal
Auditorium, a streak that included a payback defeat of Preston
Price. Interest in boxing was high in New Orleans in those
days, and Alvin had the kind of mix-it-up style that most fight
fans prefer. By 1968, he had become a ten-round fighter and a
favorite with the large fight crowds that came regularly to the
Auditorium, which stands near the French Quarter.

His second loss came in his first fight on the road, a
decision to a tough veteran, Willie Crosby of Mobile. Although
Crosby had beaten Alvin decisively, in Alvin's next outing

his manager, Collis's revered white friend Mike Cusimano, arranged a good opportunity for him as a late substitute in a main event in Kansas City against the well-known New Yorker Bobby Harrington. "WILL ACCEPT FIGHT WITH HARRINGTON," Mike wired the promoter. "YOUR CLUB—NOVEMBER 12, 1968 165 POUNDS $350 FLAT—TWO EXCURSION RATE ROUND TRIP PLANE TICKETS AND HOTEL ACCOMMODATIONS SEND CONTRACT." Mike accompanied Alvin to Kansas City, where he fought well but was denied the decision in a ten-round draw.

His visibility as a boxer now made it possible for him to move from Woodward, Wight to a better-paying job in the mayonnaise and condiment plant beneath the huge neon "B-l-u-e P-l-a-t-e" sign that still sparkles every night in the middle of town on Jeff Davis Parkway.

At Blue Plate he worked his way up to operating the steam-capping machine, which stamped lids on jars of preserves. His supervisor there, John Lincks, remembered him to me as "a very good worker." He said Alvin sometimes brought boxing posters to tape up around the plant, and often, the day after a fight, would come to work "all beat up."

Alvin's most active year in the ring was 1969. In that year, in which he still worked at Blue Plate, he fought eight times, seventy-seven rounds, headlining five cards at the Auditorium and winning twice out of town—in Baton Rouge and Corpus Christi. In July he took on Eddie Pace, whom top middleweights and many light heavies were ducking. When I asked Tony Licata about Alvin's fight with Pace, he commented that "Alvin could be hit. Bossman Pace hit Alvin a lot."

Others often brought up the bout with Pace, a fight that came at the midpoint of Alvin's career. The way one friend of Alvin's heard it, the fighters were supposed to go easy, but because of his "big heart" Alvin tried for a win, and Pace, a large middleweight with a large punch, "put a terrible whippin' on him" for the full ten rounds.

"He dropped dead . . . in a gym in California," Tony Licata remembered. "Bossman Pace was a hitter. . . ."

After absorbing this beating by Eddie Pace, Alvin fought again after just two weeks, winning a ten-round decision at the Auditorium. A month later, in his biggest win to that point, he decisioned Charlie Shipes, a ranked fighter. In an ambitious move near the end of the year, Mike matched him against the formidable Ralph Palladin in Baltimore. Alvin lost the decision, but the fight so pleased the crowd that the Maryland promoter offered him another fight early in 1970. His opponent, the southpaw Philadelphian Billy Lloyd, had a style Alvin never quite solved. Lloyd won a questionable split decision, but the bout was so hard fought they were rematched a month later in Louisiana.

The New Orleans promoter Lou Messina staged the rematch on April 21 at the St. Bernard Civic Auditorium in a neighboring parish, the first of Alvin's only two local fights not at the Auditorium. Although Collis often told me that he himself had "never been sick a day" in his life, his daughter Gloria said he was home in bed with the flu on this night in April. His top contender from the fifties, Charley Joseph, replaced him in Alvin's corner alongside Mike. Gloria had a seat in the front row. The fight was a repeat of Alvin and Lloyd's first one, a sustained brawl. Both fighters bled freely, but Alvin led on all cards entering the tenth. He had almost put Lloyd down in the seventh when, according to the newspaper reporter in attendance, he hit him with as many as twenty consecutive rights. But in the tenth Lloyd surged back. Near the end of the round, only seconds from the end of the fight, a long left cross dropped Alvin on his back in a corner. At first it seemed he was too hurt and fatigued to move; then, using the turnbuckles hand over hand, he pulled himself to his feet. The wild, standing crowd was divided between those shrieking for more action and those shouting for the referee to stop it. Lloyd leaped at Alvin and pounded him with lefts. The referee stepped in, seeming to call a halt, but Alvin protested. The referee moved away. Lloyd tagged him flush with another left, and Alvin went down like sand. Gloria had been beating the apron, pleading with Mike and Charley to throw in the towel. She later said she couldn't believe they made no move to end it as the count began again and once more, saggingly, Alvin commenced hauling himself up the ropes. Then, transported by the frenzy and the blood masking Alvin's face, Gloria was in the ring, a hysterical fury between the other fighter and her brother. At once handlers from both sides scrambled in, followed by small thrown objects, then a chair. Spectators swarmed toward the steps. In the confusion, reporters didn't realize that the woman, not the referee, had stopped the fight. Corroborating Gloria's version of the ending, Mike said he vaguely recalled that a woman had intervened at the end of the fight. Yes, it could have been Alvin's sister, but if so she hadn't done her brother any favor: if he had been allowed to weather the brief remainder of the round, he would have taken the decision. As it was, the referee was obliged to declare Billy Lloyd a TKO winner in 2:47 of the tenth. This was the only knockout Alvin suffered until his last fight.

From this low point he again recovered quickly. Within a month he topped another card at the Auditorium, knocking out his journeyman opponent for his twenty-second win. In July he was matched again against Willie Crosby, this time at home. Lou Messina billed it as being for the "Southern middleweight championship." This title, like the almost identical "Negro" title Collis had held in the thirties, was purely a promotional device. Although Crosby had knocked him down three times in Mobile, Alvin took charge. Wearing the black velvet trunks made for him by a friend of his wife, Diane, Alvin jabbed and moved well. From the second round on he bled from a sliced left eyelid, but he also cut Crosby, who had never been cut before, so badly that the fight had to be stopped in the sixth. In the ring afterward, Lou Messina presented Alvin with a tall trophy from Malcolm Faber's Sporting Goods and Trophy Manufacturers, the same trophy that—no matter how she rearranges the furniture—always stands prominently in the first room of Gloria's apartment.

His becoming "middleweight champ of the South" began a period of relative prosperity for Alvin, Collis, and most of the rest of the family, who were boosted by their close connection to his local success. When I met Diane in New York, she told me how, when Alvin fought at home, the adult population of the project and many others in the Seventh Ward drove to the Auditorium in noisy cavalcades. Afterward there would be celebrations lasting until early morning at the Star Lounge, which faced the project on St. Bernard. Freshly showered and well dressed, Alvin would make an appearance at the Star, set everyone up, and have a beer. Then he would take Diane to eat at Dooky Chase's, one of the very finest of the city's fine black-owned restaurants—just the two of them. When he and Diane reached home, win or lose, he would wake the children and tell them in detail about the fight. Alvin Jr. and Kevin both told me they had only pretended to sleep, lying open-eyed in the dark, listening for his step in the courtyard.

Diane also told me about a man she sometimes lived with

now in New York, a man she said she "had a baby for," but she told me this only to make the point that she had let this man know from the first that she had a husband in prison and "would hook up with him again" if he were ever freed. It would have to be like this, she said, because she had met her husband at a girlfriend's when she was "only nine." She was surprised when he liked her, because all of her girlfriends liked him. They grew so close so soon that her mother sent her away in the summers to "stay by" her father in Providence or Boston. But each time she returned it was impossible for anyone to keep her and Alvin apart. When at fifteen she became pregnant, he took it on himself to marry her, a decision some of his male friends thought strange. But during their marriage she took much on herself too: she would drive the car for his roadwork early in the morning, then take him to work, then pick him up afterward and take him to the gym, waiting while he trained, then drive him home. After she had served him dinner, he always smoked part of a cigarette, even when in training for a fight; he would "dench" it out and smoke the rest of the "dench" later when they were in bed; she would talk to him, and while she talked he would drift off to sleep.

They spent their last few frantic months together in New York. These followed his becoming hooked on heroin at the end of his boxing career and immediately preceded his extradition back to Louisiana. During these months, they would "swing"— that is, share her methadone. Since he wasn't registered in the clinic, only she could stand before the attendant and drink from the paper cup; afterward she would swing around to kiss him, and he would swallow what he needed out of her mouth. At the time I talked with her, she insisted to Connie, Alvin's sister in Harlem, that he was "better off where he is," because at least in prison there were three meals a day.

• • •

The seventies started so well for Alvin and his family that he was able to leave his job at Blue Plate and devote all his working energy to fighting. He successfully defended his Southern title twice before good houses in the

Auditorium. Then, in January 1971, Mike arranged for him to fight in Philadelphia against the knockout artist Willie "the Worm" Monroe. Monroe brought fifteen straight kayos into the fight. Alvin broke Monroe's knockout streak, but the decision went against him. It was a punishing ten rounds for both of them.

Two months later, back in New Orleans, he decisioned the longtime contender Kitten Hayward. But this victory led to no new opportunities. During the next fourteen months, he fought five times more, his last fights for his father and Mike: two on the road—in Mobile and Corpus Christi, where his bouts against tough journeymen did nothing to distinguish his record—and three in the Auditorium. Now that he had had a taste of boxing success, and now that his income was based solely on the ring, he was eager for more of the glamorous high life and especially impatient for big-money fights. He became skeptical of Mike's ability to make such fights, and he began to resent Collis's unconditional loyalty to his white friend. Alvin's oldest friend and subsequent drug-selling "podnah," Pete Cole, described how Alvin would point knowingly to the names of men he had beaten—Charlie Shipes, Kitten Hayward—printed in influential boxing magazine ratings that didn't include him, before ripping the pages in half.

His last two fights at the Auditorium were damaging brawls: a second lost decision to Willie Monroe, and a third loss to his nemesis, Billy Lloyd. The crowds loved the action, but Alvin increasingly saw these fights as little more than very painful paydays; even in training for them, he doubted their potential, under Mike and Collis's direction, to move him toward the top.

There was another factor influencing his growing cynicism about boxing: Tony Licata. They had sparred in the same gyms while gaining seasoning, but even very early on they and their handlers seemed to sense they were on a collision course—if not for the middleweight title, then for something more personal. In their first gym meetings, Alvin was more advanced than Tony, who was then still a teenager. Alvin may have tried to follow instructions and practice restraint in working with the younger man, but Tony was very aggressive and couldn't easily assume the role of apprentice. Training sessions between them turned into rounds fiercer than some fighters ever *fight*. After Tony turned pro, his trainers and Collis decided to keep him and Alvin in different gyms whenever possible. As their skills developed further, it was understood that they were not to work together.

It would have been hard for anyone in Alvin's place not to feel envy at the way influential people were grooming Tony's career. In a sequence of carefully chosen matches, Tony rang up more than twenty wins without a loss. Before he had fought anyone of the caliber of Alvin's toughest opponents, Tony had already replaced Alvin as the top draw at the Auditorium. Like Alvin, he was a crowd-pleaser with undeniable courage, but some of his other ring assets differed from Alvin's: he was a photogenic, very young white man who moved gracefully and possessed dazzling hand speed. His star rose as Alvin's seemed to stall. Soon his name appeared in various rating systems that had never given Alvin much ink.

Even though promoters and fans spoke eagerly of a Licata-Phillips fight as a natural, Tony's people had no intention of matching them until Tony was more than ready. It was no coincidence that Alvin's Southern title wasn't always on the line in the fights that followed his winning of it; the belt was being saved as added spice for his eventual meeting with Tony. So, in the spring of 1972, it must have seemed to Alvin that his only certain prospect was to continue a pattern of hard, not very profitable fighting while being denied the one good payday available to him.

"Left me lookin' like a stupid monkey, me an' Mike," was Collis's terse description of how Alvin worked out a new deal for himself with his friend, Johnny Powell, who trained for Malcolm Faber. "Come to me, aksed for his contrac'. What I'm go'n do? That was my son." The break with Mike and his father came about a month after Alvin decisioned the veteran Ernie Burns in early May in Mobile. In buying the contract, Malcolm Faber gave assurances that his next opponent would be a contender. There was also talk of a date in Madison Square Garden before Christmas.

He first fought for Malcolm Faber and Johnny Powell two months later, on August 21. Faber had brought in the seventh-ranked welterweight, Ronnie Harris, to face him at the Auditorium. Alvin came in several pounds under his usual weight and, fighting with new vigor, convincingly won almost every round. "I felt in better shape than usual," he told reporters afterward. "I'm ready for Licata. This fight was to ensure that."

Within three weeks, Faber had him fighting again at the Auditorium and for a third time against Willie Monroe, whom many top middleweights avoided. This was a popular, profitable pairing since fans vividly remembered their second fight, which had taken place at the Auditorium in January. This time Alvin stayed more on top of "the Worm," and they fought the close, feverish rounds almost entirely along the ropes. Both were punched out and near collapse at the end as the crowd stood to cheer. The split decision went to Alvin. His busy hook, and possibly the location of the fight, had made the difference and finally earned him a win over Willie Monroe.

The fight in New York came a month later. Malcolm Faber made good on his word: he had booked Alvin as a late substitute in Madison Square Garden. Alvin's opponent, Bobby Watts, a coming young fighter, trained, as Monroe did, in Philadelphia, which has the roughest gyms in the country. Watts had had just sixteen pro fights, though he had won them all, and Johnny Powell felt he could intimidate him and his manager—"It was a woman, the li'l dude had a chick for a manager!"—by telling her that he was sorry to have made the match and that he feared Alvin would hurt "her boy." In Johnny's prefight snapshots, both Watts and Alvin, who looked old and hard enough to be Watts's father, were noticeably subdued; and Watts, in fact, did look frightened. The cause of Alvin's distraction seemed less clear.

The nervousness Watts showed at the weigh-in was either a psych job of his own or something he put behind him at the opening bell. He used his greater height and reach to keep his listless opponent off balance throughout the fight, mixing flurries to the body with his steady jab and long crosses. Alvin outpunched him for about thirty seconds in the seventh. Otherwise, it was all Bobby "Boogaloo" Watts, who came back in the eighth to stagger Alvin and knock out his mouthpiece. This was the same Boogaloo Watts who remained a high-ranking contender throughout the seventies and who, during a sparring session in the eighties, broke the ribs of the great middleweight champion Marvin Hagler.

Alvin's loss in New York received scant coverage by the New Orleans media and thus did little to mute the local clamor for a fight between him and Tony Licata. Tony had been making such impressive progress that the match was agreed on shortly after Alvin and Johnny returned from New York. It took place on November 28, 1972, just after Thanksgiving. In order to accommodate an expected record crowd, the fight was held not in the Auditorium but in a larger arena, the Rivergate, a newly constructed convention hall that stands near where Canal Street meets the river.

Possibly because Tony's drawing power was certain, prefight publicity touted Alvin. In a feature story published shortly before the fight, Waddell Summers wrote that "Phillips's bouts have been marked by his super condition, his willingness to mix, his courage and his ability to take punishment and come back. He has parlayed the aforementioned assets, plus a good left hook and a great desire to win, into recognition as a foe worthy enough to challenge any top middleweight. Phillips has gained the admiration and respect of the fight crowd by his willingness to battle anyone they sent against him, regardless of reputation."

Gloria had good seats for the fight and enjoyed VIP treatment. She remembered being ushered to Alvin's dressing room during the prelims. Through a distant doorway at the end of the corridor, she saw him "on his back on a table," lying "still, still." As she leaned over to kiss him, he opened his eyes and whispered, "This is my last fight, sis."

When they entered the ring, Tony was twenty years old and undefeated in thirty-two fights. Alvin was thirty, with a record of 30-11-1. That night, both were dead game.

Afterward, the *Times-Picayune* described it as "an absolutely torrid clash from first bell to last." According to the paper and to spectators I spoke to, Tony's hand speed won the first round, but Alvin stayed busier and also outjabbed him through the middle rounds. Sensing he was behind, Tony pressed Alvin with flurries of punches in rounds nine and ten, but after each attack Alvin fought his way off the ropes.

Racial partisanship throughout the crowd mirrored the narrow advantage that sawed back and forth between the fighters. Blacks and whites alike signified and cheered aggressively each time their man scored. The 3,586 people in attendance stood through the last two rounds. They remained standing after the last bell and gave both fighters an extended ovation. When the decision was announced, an uproar ensued, and altercations between blacks and whites broke out around the arena. The referee voted for Alvin five rounds to four and scored one even; but because the two judges scored it five-five, the decision was a majority draw. (The newspaper and the consensus among boxing people at ringside favored Alvin.)

After security forces had escorted the fighters from the ring, and extra police finished calming the crowd, Tony's handlers complained of his having a weight problem. Alvin was too dejected to say much to reporters.

About two weeks after the fight with Tony Licata, Alvin went with Pete Cole to a Stevie Wonder concert at the Auditorium. "We had us a time that night," Pete remembered, shaking his head. "Everybody knew he whipped Licata. The whole place was glad to see him, us." In the course of the evening Alvin "got loaded" on heroin. They stayed up all night. Toward dawn, back in the project, they decided to go in together and sell drugs—there was no future in boxing. It seemed smarter than just buying. With Pete's experience and connections and Alvin's intimidating reputation, they felt they couldn't miss: sell a little, make a little money, and always have wholesale, high-quality product to keep them feeling good.

The rematch with Tony Licata, Alvin's last fight at home, was set for April 4, 1973—in the Auditorium, which soon sold out.

Alvin damaged one of his hands in training, but it was too late by then to postpone the show. His injury and the cortisone shots he received to blunt the pain were never made public. Prefight coverage emphasized international title prospects, the Southern title, and the fight—"a popular 'mixed match,' as they are called today"—as a rare natural pairing of evenly skilled, exciting athletes. There was also the story and interview with Collis, "A Champ at Ringside," in which Waddell Summers portrayed the father-son relationship in Alvin's boxing background while maintaining silence about the broken business relationship that had soured it. Typically, Collis's public comments skirted controversy and steered toward personal accord and tactical elements of boxing: "I don't think there's any hard feelings in this fight. The boys used to work together at one time. Tony's an awfully nice kid. His people, especially his dad, have been nice to me too. He's a fast puncher and is very game. You've got to stay on him. He don't pass up nothing."

Except briefly during the first two rounds, Alvin wasn't able to "stay on" his man. Even at the beginning, he appeared fought out. The sports page reported that "Tony consistently got off first and completely outspeeded the game Phillips." Although "both were well applauded at the end," the only similarities between Alvin's performances in April and November were his toughness and courage. Tony drew blood early and several times had Alvin on the verge of a knockdown.

It was rumored that Tony could have knocked him out but respected him too much to do it. When I asked Tony about this, he raised his hand as if to block the question. He said the rumor wasn't true. In his dressing room after the fight, Tony praised him routinely: "Alvin always comes to fight." Pressed for an explanation of his loss, Alvin tossed off an answer that suggested his frustration and a willingness to give up the battle: "My legs gave out on me after the third round. It could be age or I over-ran—or didn't run enough." He said nothing about his hand—and, naturally, nothing about his habit.

European closes are common to the careers of many once potent American fighters. On June 2 came the end-of-the-road meeting with European champ Jean-Claude Bouttier in Monte Carlo. Ten thousand people paid to enter the Louis II soccer stadium to see Emile Griffith, in his twenty-first title fight, unsuccessfully challenge Carlos Monzon in the main event. Except for his slack effort against Bouttier, Alvin must have had a good time, maybe the time of his life, in Italy and Monaco. He had traveled far, and he had worked with Griffith and would remember him as a friend. Bouttier went on to a title shot, and a decision loss, against Monzon in September in Paris. Alvin flew home to the project, in his own words to Pete, a "universal citizen."

Two summers later, Tony had his shot at the title, and Monzon praised his bravery after knocking him out in the tenth round in Madison Square Garden. By then, Alvin was in jail, awaiting trial.

• • •

Now, in Angola, it was unusually hard to see him as simply real. With teeth missing in places and hair gone in the front, he wore baggy denims and a plain white T-shirt that fit him, except across his wide shoulders, the way a father's garment fits a young son.

When I asked if my letter of self-introduction had reached him, he began to speak in soft-voiced, fast, repetitious, whispery riffs, as if only to himself. Frequently he paused, stuttering, to take issue with what he had just said, correcting himself in fragmented phrases. Yes, he allowed, staring in annoyed wonderment at the hand I had touched, he *had* received a letter, but he couldn't understand it. It was written funny, and his mind was "jammed up, too jammed up—jammed up, like in *J*, Camp *J*, this is *lock-down*, Camp *J*, where I live."

I tried to explain what I had said in the letter: my interest in his father and his family and the project I had undertaken—to write about them.

"Yeh, well," he interrupted, speaking louder, "a book can be *up*, a book can be *down*. Book can be a lift. Like my hand there. *You see my hand!?*" His slack left arm appeared to levitate, his ringless, tattooed fingers—L-O-V-E—drifting vertically along the bars. "Or a book can look like a lift and still be a jam. Bible's the only book I read now. The Bible's a lift, the Bible's a *jam*."

Hoping to put him at least somewhat at ease, I made the mistake of showing him the contract Collis and I had had drawn up. He took it and held it on his side of the bars and looked at it for a long time, shaking his head. I tried to explain how well I understood the irony of this contract in relation to the problems caused by boxing contracts in his past. I labored to make him see that I was aware of all that. This one would be different: Collis or his heirs would receive fifty percent of any profit that a book about them might earn—if such a book materialized. It was now illegal for it to be otherwise. (I cringed at the lameness of my phrases.)

But he paid me little mind. More agitated than before, he spoke so quickly and softly I could scarcely follow him. It seemed he was talking about jewelry. At first this was all I could gather. I listened in nervous bafflement as the words "emerald" and "diamond" kept coming back.

"My wife was a diamond," he said, as if the transition were obvious. "That's what I always told her."

Then he was talking about one of his sons, the last of six

children his wife had had by him, a child who was the congenitally handicapped brother of a stillborn twin.

The family used different names when speaking of this son, who—though Alvin didn't know it—was now, by necessity, in a foster home somewhere in New York.

Jude: Gloria eventually told me that this was his last son's name. "After the saint," she said, "St. Jude, the one for trouble that's hopeless." But the girlfriend of one of Alvin's brothers would later tell me, no, this was wrong, the child was named Julius—after Alvin and Diane's old friend Pete, who would allow, when I met him the following spring, that this *was* possible, since his own given name was Junius Pierre Cole III. But on one point everyone agreed: Alvin had named the twins on his own. Diane said she had thought up enough names for babies. That was before she had left New Orleans, after a minor drug charge, for her present life in Harlem.

"Words will run," Alvin whispered now, looking down toward the base of the bars, "Names run, don't they?"

Though he continued to talk of "precious stones . . . jewels," I still didn't understand. It would be more than a year before, casting back over this part of the day as I often did, I suddenly would see it: "jewels." Jules! He had named his son Jules.

It was "like precious stones," he said again. The year Jules was born, the Beatles had that song, "Hey, Jude." "And that was like 'Lucy in the Sky.' You know, 'Lucy in the Sky . . . with Diamonds.' " And his ex-manager Mike Cusimano had an address that appealed to him. "Mist' Cusimano stays in that big house on Emerald Street." He said it evenly, but also as if he were cursing. " 'Bout big as this paper here." He handed back the contract and the letterhead envelope bearing the name of the law firm of Mike's son Sal. "You know Mist' Cusimano? You been to his house on Emerald Street? Maybe you work for him. I worked for him. I—"

He stepped back from the bars. Three guards had entered the corridor and, bickering and chuffing, now trotted toward us. I heard the tallest one tell the others to take me out quickly. They put their hands around my arms. They would have to move us, the tallest one said, to a regular visiting area. But first— and here he produced a document—Alvin would have to sign a publicity release. He stuck the form and a pen through the bars.

"Yes, suh. Yes, suh," Alvin said, in what sounded to me like a parody of slavishness.

When I said, no, he needn't agree against his will, he only shook his head.

"I signs all the papers," he said. "It's like a contract."

He scrawled his name, and, while the tallest guard opened the cell, he turned around like an obedient child and put the insides of his wrists together behind his back, holding them away from his body so one of the other guards could more easily bracelet them with handcuffs.

Flanking his shoulders, the first two guards steered him out of the cell. The third guard and I waited for them to wheel by; then we fell in behind, lurched forward, and became a procession.

Every prisoner now lay so his opened eyes could track us the width of his cell. Alvin walked meekly between the guards, his ears about level with their shoulders. The heels of his shower thongs snapped at his overlong pant cuffs. It wasn't until we had all moved clumsily through the slowly opened sequence of doors and were outside that I was able to read the very small letters—R-O-C-K—written in nail polish across the back of his T-shirt.

I stepped to the side of him as we waited for the door to a visiting cell farther down the walk to be unlocked from within. It was a cloudless afternoon. Sunlight glinted on the chain-link fences beyond and shone beautifully on fertile fields rippling in the distance. In a gun tower between the fences, one of Angola's female sharpshooters appeared in silhouette through a window framed in print kitchen curtains. She chatted into a telephone receiver and stroked the underside of her puffed hive of hair.

The bright light disclosed the full extent of Alvin's newly receded hairline and the blurred margins of the greenish jailhouse-tattooed letters on his sallow brown arms: D-I-A-N-E and (his first two sons) A-L-V-I-N and K-E-V-I-N. It was easy to study him now because, as we waited, he paid no evident attention to the guards or to me. His eyes roamed the distant grass and sky. He could have been any man standing idly alone, surveying his natural surroundings. Breeze ruffled his denims and loose T-shirt. "Rock," the small word on the cotton across his shoulder blades, seemed a persistent, if frail, contradiction of Alan Citron's portrait of him as a frightened, broken man. Even when trained down into fighting shape, Alvin had been a full-bodied middleweight who, in gyms, had walked through large light heavies. Now he was smaller than I was and weighed, at the most, maybe 140.

When the door at last opened, I glimpsed another cellblock. A prisoner walking there called out, "Say, Al-*vin!*" in an eager, pleased way that made me think they hadn't seen each other in a long time. Alvin scarcely nodded, for at the first clatch of the tumblers in the lock, he had become attentive to the guards, and when one of them touched him, he at once stepped inside.

The tallest guard, the pale one with the acne, sullenly guided me to the second door and shut me in in a small, dim visiting room. The space was empty except for a straight chair. Doubled steel mesh formed a panel in one wall. Above me, its blades stalled, a shorted-out ventilator hummed. The door, which stood crooked on its hinges, grated on the gritty cement, then slammed behind me. A key turned the complaining tumblers back into place.

Beyond the panel was a space identical to mine and also furnished with a chair. Because of the motionless air and extreme heat, my shirt was soaked through by the time the door opened on Alvin's side. His wrists were now cuffed in front of him. He sat down at some distance from the screen and began speaking right away.

"Was married when I was seventeen. Have a wife and six children in New Orleans. I tell my children to stay in school and make between forty and a hundred on the cards. They don't do it, don't do it right, I whip 'em, tear 'em up! But they gotta eat. That's what I tell 'em. *Eat!*"

Misaligned gaps in the doubled mesh made his image waver before me. If I had still hoped our conversation might loosely follow the pattern of an interview, that hope now vanished. He spoke on, compulsively and insistently, in low whispers that I couldn't always clearly hear. It was obvious that he wouldn't address whatever it was I had thought I wanted to learn. He would talk, as he said, "till the time is gone," and I would strain forward in the chair opposite him, trying to catch the meaning that might lie in his words and in his alternately mocking and humble inflections.

"Down time," he said quickly, his head bowed toward his chest. "This is down time. Like a strip-down, a jam, all the things been jammed in my head—like they was jammed in backwards. Backwards and down. It all presses down to the feet, but can't go no further 'cause nothin's under there but concrete and rock. Yeh, concrete and rock, that's right. Well, a diamond's harder than a rock, but I still remember how to use my feet."

He paused for possibly a minute, then asked if I had seen Jimmy Carter in New Orleans. I said I had not.

He seemed agitated. "Wh-what? You mean the . . . the . . . the President didn't come to Louisiana?"

When I said I didn't think so, he accused me of misleading him. "You say the President didn't come to Louisiana? You must be playin' with my head. You could do it too, ex-fighter, ex-junkie's got a head easy to play with. But I know *Louisiana*, it's the bottom, and the shit's go'n fall on everybody!"

Not knowing how to answer his bitterness, I asked if I could ask him a question.

"*Shoot!*" he shouted immediately and in a way that made me think of the multiple implications, which seemed deliberate in many of his phrases.

Supposing the memory might be more pleasant to him, I brought up his trip to the Riviera with his other trainer, Johnny Powell. I asked how it had been, traveling and training in Europe before his last fight.

He whispered to himself for a few moments, then his voice gradually rose: "Monte Carlo, San Remo, the racetrack, casinos, that smelled pretty good, smelled better than Louisiana, better than New Orleans, better than Carter and the Kennedys, *all* a the Kennedys."

He raised his head to peer at me for the first time. Because of the doubled screen, I couldn't look at both of his eyes at once.

"If I was to tell you the moon is green—" He stopped himself and dropped his eyes.

As if finally stifled by the heat, we sat for a moment in silence except for the audible current in the broken ventilator.

"I'm not in my right head," he continued apologetically. "Been goin' through these changes, can't keep a thought straight, nuttin' up." Now he shouted: *"I'm nuttin' up!"*

After another silence, he mentioned headaches. He seemed to be referring both to physical pain and to my visit's causing him problems with other convicts who might think that he was gaining something worth trying to take from him. I asked if he preferred for me just to leave him alone. His response was incoherent, and abruptly he began talking about boxing.

"That ring," he said. "That's what you want to hear about, I know that's it, that must be it— What was we speakin' of now . . . ? Wait . . . here it come, here it come round again: that ring. That ring's cold as ice. Hot ice. Emile Griffith, Gil Clancy, Carlos Monzon, the Garden. That ring's a mystery, you got all types a rings around it. You got ten-round, eight-, six-, you got four-round fighters, two-round fighters—that's right, you b'lieve it, *two*-round—you got amateurs, got people whose daddies help 'em just put a foot in it, people who make a safe livin' off a makin' fights, other people who write about it . . . 'Scuse me, you hafta excuse me. My mind's not right."

I asked if he knew of a way I could help him.

"What do I need?" he snapped. "What I need? I need some eyeglasses, I need me some specs to talk about that ring."

He went on at a rushing pace I couldn't follow. Then I made out one muttered phrase: "Fat butt." I thought he was referring to his last opponent, Jean-Claude Bouttier, the European Champion. But he said, no, that it was only like Bouttier— "practically the same name as him"—and that he was thinking about Joe Bordelon, a man who managed the Circle Drugstore, which stood on St. Bernard Avenue across from the project. Implying he had stolen from Bordelon's store as a child, he spoke savagely and said the man "had a fat butt and was never nice to kids!"

In futility I looked at the sheaf of sweat-smudged notes and questions in my lap. He continued talking into his chest too softly and too fast for me to make out the rest of his words. Suddenly my eyes stung, and I kept my head down so that, even if he looked at me, he wouldn't be able to tell they had teared over. I had been wrong in thinking myself prepared for this visit. "What's it *like?*" I blurted, as if angry, interrupting his low, running murmur. "What do you *do*, just in that cell twenty-three hours a day!?"

"Oh, I travel," he answered distinctly and at once. "At night I drive all over New Orleans, my home. Been to New York. Rome. London. But it all comes back home. Home to the Seventh Ward, where I come up. Yeh, nights I drive up on Canal Street. Then around on the Lakefront, Ponchartrain Park. Then back down St. Bernard." He whispered confidentially. "I just leave a small flame burnin'. I cut across the courtyard and watch for the broken step . . . Then I go in and check the stove to see that that small flame's still lit. I turn it down if I have to. That's where I go at night. That's where I live."

Current pulsed into the ventilator, then ceased.

I don't know how much later it was when someone rapped on the door. Although I was wary of false hope—for either of us—I quickly ventured that what I wrote might improve things for him and the rest of the family.

He sneered. "What you wanna play with my head for? Words run. Cain't no *book* do nothin'."

Standing, I said I didn't think his crime deserved its punishment and that, even if I was wrong, he still didn't belong in a place like Angola.

He looked up, the doubled mesh making his neck appear to have seams. "Yeh, well," he answered, "if I don't belong here, I guess they's maybe a thousand like me don't belong here either." He said something more, a gush of words, as the door was dredged open and a guard spoke to me sharply.

Moving toward the bright doorway, I raised my hand in a subdued wave. Beyond the screen, he mimicked my gesture exactly. On the walkway, I turned and looked back inside. He was a blurred silhouette on the panel. A tepid breeze felt cool on my wet clothes. I raised my hand again, and he did exactly the same as the guard lunged on the heavy door, slamming it between us.

All the guards now stared at me, and the pale one with the acne began to question why, earlier, I had complicated their jobs by entering a part of the prison I must have realized was forbidden me. Although I looked attentively up at him, at his poor ravaged skin, I was still hearing the last things Alvin had said.

"You see my wife and children back in New Orleans, you tell 'em you saw me, just say I'm still sittin' here, say '*Al's alive,*' tell 'em I miss 'em, tell 'em I love 'em, words run, don't they, *my wife was a diamond.*"

Der Morgen

Im Herbst da reiht der
                    Feenwind
da sich im Schnee die
Mähnen treffen.
Amseln pfeifen heer
im Wind und fressen.

Heimweh

Ich habe nicht nur Heimweh,
sondern sogar mehr. Das Heimweh
ist eine Qual außerstande.
Man kann die Auswärtigkeit
nicht aushalten. Ich
möchte gerne heim.

Morning

In Fall the wraithwind
                    turns out
for in the snow
manes are colliding.
Blackbirds pipe up a horde
in the wind and feed.

Homesickness

I'm not just homesick,
but even more. Homesickness
is a torture out of place.
The outwardness is
unbearable. I
want to go home.

Der Traum

Der Traum war um Mitternacht-.
als ich gerade tief im Schlafe war,
fuhr ich mit 2 Rössern im Trabe eine
Strasse hinauf. Der Pferde pusteten.
Ich traf im Straßenzuge einige
Buben. Schnell flogen die Häuser
vorbei. Der eine war mir nahe
und trieb meine Sehenskraft gegen
meine Seele. Die Sonne schien.
die Schnell in die Ruhe zurück-
fuhr und ich erwachte.

The Dream

The dream was at midnight-.
while I was deep in sleep,
I drove with 2 steeds at a trot up a
street. The horses panting.
In the avenue I met some
boys. Quickly the houses flew
by. And one was near me
he shoved my sight against
my soul. The sun was shining.
that quick turned back
into calm and I awoke.

Das Eichkätzchen

Im Wald und auf der Heide,
da fand ich meine Freude.
Der Förster schrack zusammen,
als es auf dem Baume war, das Eichkätzchen.
Es sprang von Alles zum Ast.
und schmor zusammen. Der
Förster fror. Und sein Gewehr.
Der Förster sah wie es gerade schah
und stach im in das Fell und fiel
vom Baume wie der Schnee.
Das Eichkätzchen hatte ein semi-
Fell von braunen Zar. Das Fell war
                                    well.
Der Fuchs sah hin und wieder und
fraß es auf. Das Essen holen. Das
Eichkätzchen war tot. Der Fuchs war
lang. wie der Förster sein Gewehr
und schoß. Er traf es nicht.

The Squirrel

In forest and in thicket,
there did I find my joy.
The ranger panicked
when it was on the tree, the squirrel.
It leapt from now to bough.
and flows together. The
ranger froze. And his gun.
The ranger shah just how it came about
and stuck in into his fur and fell
from the tree like snow.
The squirrel had a semi-
fur of brown czar. The fur was
                    whir.
The fox saw now and again and
gobbled it up. Getting dinner. The
squirrel was dead. The fox was
long. as the ranger his gun
and shot. He missed.

Translated by Melissa Monroe

Jean Tinguely
Printed silk scarf, 1978
14 x 40 in.

Each cover of *Grand Street* features an actual-size detail of a chosen artwork. The entire work is reproduced at left. An enlarged detail from the same work appears on the title page. A portfolio of Jean Tinguely's work from 1954 to 1988 begins on page 62.

Indran Amirthanayagam comes from Sri Lanka. His poems have appeared in *The Kenyon Review*, *The Massachusetts Review*, *Bomb*, *The Portable Lower East Side*, and other journals. His first collection, *The Elephants of Reckoning* (Hanging Loose Press), will appear in the fall of 1992.

Rae Armantrout published two books of poems in 1991: *Necromance* (Sun and Moon) and *Couverture*, a volume of selected poems translated into French by Denis Dormoy (Les Cahiers de Royaumont). Her work has recently appeared in *Conjunctions*. She teaches writing at the University of California in San Diego.

Randolph Bates teaches expository writing at Harvard University. "Natural Life" is an excerpt from his forthcoming book *Rings: On the Life and Family of a Southern Fighter*, to be published by Farrar, Straus & Giroux in May 1992.

Nina Berberova was born in St. Petersburg in 1901. She left Russia in 1922 and, three years later, settled in Paris, where she soon became a central figure in the Russian émigré community. In 1950 she moved to the United States, where she still lives. "The Disappearance of the Turgenev Library" is a translation of *Konets Tourguenevskoï biblioteki*.

Andrei Bitov was born in 1937 in Leningrad, where he studied geological research at the Mining Institute. Since 1963, he has devoted himself entirely to writing. "History Lesson" is from *A Captive of the Caucasus*, to be published in June by Farrar, Straus & Giroux. Other works by Bitov in English translation are a novel, *Pushkin House*, and a collection of stories, *Life in Windy Weather*.

Louise Bourgeois was born in 1911 in Paris, where she studied at the Ecole du Louvre and the Ecole des Beaux-Arts. She has lived in New York since 1938. Her paintings and sculpture have been exhibited worldwide and can currently be seen at the Museum of Modern Art and the British Museum, among many others. She is represented by the Robert Miller Gallery.

Susan Brownsberger holds degrees from Radcliffe College and Boston College. In addition to *A Captive of the Caucasus* and Bitov's novel *Pushkin House*, she has translated works by Yuz Aleshkovsky, Vladimir Voinovich, and Fazil Iskander. She is currently working on the translation of Bitov's newest book, *The Ark*.

Clayton Eshleman's most recent books include *Hotel Cro-Magnon* (1989), *Antiphonal Swing* (1989), *Novices* (1989), and *Conductors of the Pit* (1988). He teaches at Eastern Michigan University, where he edits *Sulfur* magazine.

Jonathan Galassi has translated a selection of Montale's essays, *The Second Life of Art* (1982), and a volume of his late poems, *Otherwise: Last and First Poems* (1984). He is currently completing a translation of Montale's major poetry.

Ernst Herbeck (1920–1991), who has been called "probably Austria's most important postwar poet," spent most of his adult life in the Artists' House of the Psychiatric and Neurological Hospital at Klosterneuburg. Dr. Leo Navratil of that institution has been responsible for the publication of Herbeck's work. The four poems here are from Herbeck's selected poems, *Alexander* (1982), and are reprinted by permission of Residenz Verlag, Salzburg and Vienna.

Pierre Joris has published twenty books of poetry, most recently *Turbulence* (Saint Lazare Press) and *The Irritation Ditch* (Parenthesis Writing Series), as well as several anthologies and many volumes of translations. He is working with Jerome Rothenberg on a two-volume global anthology of twentieth-century avant-garde poetry for publication by the University of California.

Mary-Claire King is Professor of Genetics and of Epidemiology at the University of California at Berkeley. She is interested in the genetics of complex traits, including breast cancer, inherited deafness, autoimmunity, and human diversity. She and her daughter Emily live in Berkeley.

Kenneth Koch's "The First Step," inspired by trips to China in 1984 and 1991, is the title poem of his new book of poems, to be published next year. A book of stories, *Hotel Lambosa,* will also be published in 1993. Recent books include *One Thousand Avant-Garde Plays* (1988) and a British *Selected Poems* (Carcanet, 1991).

David Mamet received the 1984 Pulitzer Prize and the New York Drama Critics Circle Award for his play *Glengarry Glen Ross.* He is the author of a dozen other plays and seven screenplays (most recently *Homicide*). His other writings include a book for children with drawings by Donald Sultan, two volumes of essays, and a collection of poems, *The Hero Pony.* He has also directed two films and translated the works of Anton Chekhov and Pierre Laville.

Herbert Woodward Martin recently completed a video anthology of the poems of Paul Laurence Dunbar: *The Eyes of the Poet.* He is poet in residence at the University of Dayton, Ohio.

Arthur Miller's "Homely Girl, A Life" is the opening section of a novella, also called "Homely Girl." The complete text will be published in a special first edition, with images by Louise Bourgeois, in May 1992 by Peter Blum Edition (New York). It is one of a series of stories about people in the years of the Great Depression on which Miller has been periodically working.

Melissa Monroe lives and teaches in Boston.

Eugenio Montale was born in Genoa in 1896 and died in Milan in 1981. He received the Nobel Prize for Literature in 1976. Montale's "Motets," which he later referred to as a *romanzetto autobiografico,* or autobiographical novelette, date from the 1930s. They form a key element of his second collection of poems, *Le occasioni* (*The Occasions*), published in 1939.

Ben Okri is a Nigerian writer who lives in London. He has won several prizes, including the *Paris Review* Aga Khan prize for fiction and, most recently, the 1991 Booker Prize for Fiction for his novel *The Famished Road* (which will be published in the United States by Doubleday in May). Okri's volume of stories *Incidents at the Shrine* was published in Britain by William Heinemann Ltd., but has not yet been published in the United States.

Julio Ortega, originally from Trujillo, Peru, is a Professor in the Spanish Department at Brown University. He has published poetry, fiction, and essays, and most recently has edited a critical edition of *Trilce* (Cátedra, Madrid, 1991).

Kit Robinson's most recent books are *Counter Meditation* (Zasterle Press, 1991) and *The Champagne of Concrete* (Potes and Poets, 1991). He resides in Berkeley and is currently working on the translation from the Russian of a long poem by the Ukrainian Ilya Kutik.

Jerome Rothenberg is the author of more than fifty books of poetry, the latest of which, *Khurbn & Other Poems*, was recently published by New Directions. His experimental anthologies of traditional and contemporary poetry include *Technicians of the Sacred* (University of California Press) and *Shaking the Pumpkin* (University of New Mexico Press).

Kurt Schwitters was born in Hannover in 1887. He was conventionally trained as a visual artist, but soon began to create radically original works in many media. His work, to which he gave the name of *Merz*, had close affinities with Dada, as well as with Dutch and Russian Constructivism. Schwitters published a magazine (*Merz*), gave poetry readings and performances throughout Europe, and mapped out a series of "total art works." After being forced into exile by the Nazis, he lived in Norway and then in England, where he died in 1948. "The Onion" will be included in *PPPPPP: Poems Performance Pieces Proses Plays Poetics*, a book of selected writings of Schwitters that is forthcoming from Temple University Press later this year.

Lucius Annaeus Seneca, born in Cordoba, Spain, around 4 B.C., was tutor and then advisor to the emperor Nero. Of his tragedies, which were the models for the early English dramatists, T. S. Eliot remarks: "When an Elizabethan hero or villain dies, he usually dies in the odor of Seneca." "On Cithaeron" is the first scene of the Senecan fragment *The Phoenician Women.*

David R. Slavitt's latest book is *Virgil* (Yale University Press); his *Seneca: The Tragedies, Volume I* will appear in April as part of the Johns Hopkins University Press publication of *The Complete Roman Drama in Translation*, of which he and Palmer Bovie are coeditors.

Bruce Smith is the author of two books of poems, *The Common Wages* and *Silver and Information.*

Patsy Southgate is a writer living in East Hampton, New York. She has translated works by Jean Genet, Marguerite Duras, Jean-Paul Sartre, Alain Robbe-Grillet, Bertrand Blier, and François Truffaut, among others. Her poems, short stories, and translations have appeared in *Evergreen Review, Esquire, Paris Review, Playboy,* and *Tri-Quarterly.*

Jean Tinguely's prodigious oeuvre comprises hundreds of drawings, sculptures, constructions, and performance works. Since 1954 his work has been exhibited around the world, including major retrospectives at the Jewish Museum, New York (1965), the Palazzo Grassi, Venice (1987), and the Centre Georges Pompidou, Paris (1988). His public commissions include works in Stockholm, Paris, Zurich, and Columbus (Indiana).

César Vallejo (b. Santiago de Chuco, Peru, 1892; d. Paris, France, 1938) published *Trilce,* his second book, in 1922. It consists of 77 poems and is considered to be the most radical book of poetry in the Spanish language. The Eridanos Library will publish the Eshleman/Ortega translation bilingually in 1992.

Dominique Wade was born in France in 1960 and lived in Angola from 1984 to 1989. Her photographs of that country have been exhibited there and at the Galerie Urbi et Orbi in Paris; they have been published in *Liberation, Photography, Africa International,* and other magazines.

cover & title page Jean Tinguely, printed silk scarf. Private collection. Photograph by George Hixson.

pp. 10, 19 Photographs by George Hixson.

p. 34 Photographs of the Lanuscou house (with accompanying article describing "battle") and Laura Estela Carlotto. Courtesy of Mary-Claire King and the Grandmothers of the Plaza de Mayo.

p. 36 Matilde Lanuscou's socks and pacifier, retrieved from her grave. Courtesy of Mary-Claire King and the Grandmothers.

p. 38 "Tree of Subversion." Courtesy of Mary-Claire King and the Grandmothers.

p. 39 Grandmothers of the Plaza de Mayo marching in Buenos Aires in 1979. Courtesy of Mary-Claire King and the Grandmothers.

p. 42 "We are searching for two generations": photographs from the office wall of the Grandmothers of the Plaza de Mayo. Courtesy of Mary-Claire King and the Grandmothers.

p. 44 Paula Logares. Courtesy of Mary-Claire King and the Grandmothers.

p. 50 Family tree depicting inheritance of mitochondrial DNA; mitochondrial DNA sequences of individuals from different families. Courtesy of Mary-Claire King and the Grandmothers.

pp. 62, 65–70, 72–80 Jean Tinguely, installation views and documentary photographs (titles p. 81) from the retrospective exhibition "Tinguely," Centre Georges Pompidou, Musée National d'Art Moderne, Paris. The Menil Collection, Houston.

p. 71 Jean Tinguely, poster maquette. Photograph courtesy of Jean-Yves Mock, Paris.

p. 94 Eugène Atget, *Rue de la Bûcherie*, 1902–03, albumen-silver print, 9⅜ x 7 in. The domed building is the former Faculté de Médecine, where the Turgenev Library was housed. Courtesy of The Museum of Modern Art, New York, Abbott-Levy Collection. Partial gift of Shirley C. Burden.

p. 104 *Oedipus and the Sphinx* (detail of Greek sarcophagus), c. 3rd-2nd century B.C. National Archeological Museum, Athens. Photograph courtesy of CM Dixon.

pp. 118, 124 Photographs by Inge Morath. Courtesy of the artist and Magnum Photos.

pp. 131–41, 143 Louise Bourgeois, *Anatomy*, 1990, boxed portfolio of eleven prints and one multiple. Courtesy of the artist and Peter Blum Edition, New York. Photographs by Paul Hester.

ILLUSTRATIONS

p. 148 Armenian *khatchkar.*
Photograph by Sam Sweezy.

p. 155 The Holy See of the
Armenian Apostolic Church,
Echmiadzin. Photograph by
Sam Sweezy.

p. 166 Kurt Schwitters,
cover illustration for *Anna
Blume: Dichtungen*, 1919,
photolithograph, 8⅝ x 5¾ in.
The Menil Collection, Houston.

pp. 171, 174 (detail) Kurt
Schwitters, second and seventh
illustrations for *Die Kathedrale,*
1920, photolithographs,
8⅝ x 5¾ in. The Menil
Collection, Houston.

pp. 177, 180–90 Dominique
Wade, twelve photographs
(titles p. 191), 1989. Courtesy
of the artist and Galerie Urbi et
Orbi, Paris.

pp. 192, 198, 203 Willie
Crosby and Alvin Phillips.
Photograph courtesy of the *New
Orleans Times-Picayune.*

p. 231 Poster fragment from
lower Manhattan, 1991.